According to the Pattern

By Clarence Summy

© Copyright 1992 — Clarence Summy

All rights reserved. This book is protected under the copyright laws of the United States of America. This book may not be copied or reprinted for commercial gain or profit. Short quotations or occasional page copying for personal or group study is permitted and encouraged. Permission will be granted upon request. Scripture quotations are individually identified by the appropriate Bible version initials.

Take note that the name satan and related names are not capitalized. We choose not to acknowledge him, even to the point of violating grammatical rules.

Companion Press
P.O. Box 310
Shippensburg, PA 17257-0310

"Good Stewards of the
Manifold Grace of God"

ISBN 1-56043-512-7

For Worldwide Distribution
Printed in the U.S.A.

Contents

Chapter		Page
	Preface	v
	History or His Story in Perspective	viii
1	God's Pattern: The Blueprint for Blessing	1
2	After the Pattern	15
3	Paul: A Man of Destiny	25
4	"Born Again"	39
5	One More Adam	47
6	The Messages of John	53
7	In the World	61
8	Choices for the Church	69
9	Macrocosm Ravished—Microcosm Revived	77
10	Out of Touch with Bible Reality	85
11	A Return to God's Pattern	101
12	This Your Day	109
13	Two Men on a Mission	115
14	Speak Up, Church.	131
15	Where Is the Church?	141
	The Severity of Jesus' Reprimand (Judgments)	155

Preface

The prayer of the writer is that the end product be the epitome of the inner person. The expectation would be that the theme energizes the reader, and further, says effectually to the reader: Listen to me!

In the fifteenth year of this twentieth century in the third month on the seventh day, this writer was introduced into this world as the firstborn among five children, and was majestically presided over by God-fearing, Bible-believing and church-going parents.

This was a time in history when America was looking out upon a troubled world, one about to erupt into what was later referred to as World War I; the war to end all wars.

At the turn of the century around 1898, a Jew, Theodor Herzl, by name, espoused and championed with vigor, on Israel's behalf, the *cause celebre*: a homeland as promised to Abraham by covenant.

The Balfour Declaration of 1917 declared this proposition as beneficial and incremental to world stability. This people Israel, who had been denied access to the land for several centuries, were calling upon the nations of the world to give them back their land, the Promised Land. Little time would elapse before the infamous British White Papers of 1922 would be propagated, whereby the land would be decimated by nearly 75 percent from that intent expressed in the Balfour Declaration.

This alteration inaugurated another war, the second world war, which ended in the tragic and merciless slaughter known as the holocaust. It is a period in history fraught with problems to the present day; and Israel is involved.

So many times I have reflected on Esther 4:14 (NAS), in Mordecai's encouraging as well challenging words to Queen Esther. My mother, as Esther, could hardly be called a talkative lady, but rather a lady with great intuition and devotion to the things of God.

For a long time my name "Clarence" was not significant until one day, while I was browsing in a bookstore on the lower East Side of New York City, owned by an orthodox rabbi, I came upon a book of names that was Jewish/English, English/Jewish. In it I found a startling revelation. My name translated from the Hebrew into English means "God's crown". My middle name, "Ira", was the name borne by three of King David's favorite officers.

As events unfolded in my life after my conversion, the contacts I had and the help I received in teaching Sunday School classes; my pastorate in several churches; and my relationships at Moody Bible, Winona Lake School of Theology and Lancaster School of the Bible as a member of the staff have been blessings. The relationships with giants in the ministry like Dr. William Pettingill; Dr. Frank Torrey; Henry J. Heydt, Th.D.; Dr. Joseph Hoffman Cohn; Dr. Wilbur M. Smith and a host of others of equal stature have blessed my life immeasurably as well.

My prayer is that this book will reveal that inner person to be none other than the Holy Spirit.

Bless the Lord, O my soul!

Opening Remarks

History or His Story in Perspective

The tendency of Christians has for too long been to invest too much confidence in outward appearances. The idea abroad today is that the Kingdom of God is all of a carnal nature. Forms and ceremonies ritualize in cosmetic fashion the profound aspects of the Kingdom.

All prophecies referred to, as well as many other passages in Scripture, begin with God's concern for man and for His desire to have a lasting fellowship or relationship with man.

The Kingdom of God, a concept of God, insists that it must have its beginning with us, in the inner life, and must rule there because all outward actions are to flow in conformity with the revealed and written teachings and commands of God. That is verily the Spirit of prophecy (Rev. 19:10; 2 Pet. 1:20).

The Holy Spirit will use the natural organs of speech when He controls all the faculties of life, resulting sometimes in real ecstasy, without loss of consciousness, though cut off for the time from external relations.

Of first and greatest importance to all believers is the fact that prophecy has enduring reference to the present, to the future as also to the past, and that it does have respect for the whole empire of man.

Although prophecy calls attention to individuals and to nations, it often has reference to doctrines and principles, and in this light believers in God are the impelling force, the percussion instruments, of prophecy with biblical precepts.

The Torah, also referenced as the Tanach for the entirety of the Hebrew Bible, unfolds the message of every prophet. The apostles quote liberally from the prophets in their messages and writings. The Torah and all the Bible rest heavily on and pronounce condemnation freely upon the disobedient as well as blessings on the faithful.

That was and is the principle upon which the covenant of inheritance was made with Abraham and with David in the Davidic document and in perpetuity.

Thus all the promises, whether political, ethical, judicial or ritual, rest on the inerrancy of God's Word. In short, the entirety of biblical administration finds in the prophetic vision its authority to regulate human life, commencing in the inner life and working outward until the outward is like the inward. Thus it advances from individuals on to nations. "The entrance of thy words giveth light" (Ps. 119:130a KJV). The idiom of the Hebrew suggests that the door is always open and that there are no windows. His commandments are a lamp, and teaching is light (see Proverbs 6:23).

The Messianic prophecy has no other justification than that. On it rests the Church; on that rests the glory of the Kingdom of God on earth.

The nations of the world have been given to idolatry, and are tiring of placing their confidence in and dependence on gods that do not help them in the hour of danger. The call is going out that they want a God who can help and who will answer their pleas.

The Church must be of good cheer and be strong with its message to those without hope, with the message of faith for those unfamiliar with it and with news of the covenant-keeping God whose promises are yea and amen.

1

God's Pattern: The Blueprint for Blessing

Our churches today are either unaware of the deterioration of the apostolic faith or, if aware of this profanation, do not know what to do about it, despite the clear and unmistakable warnings to the Ephesian and Thessalonian churches: "Let no one deceive you with empty words, for because of these things the wrath of God comes..." and "Let no one deceive you by any means..." (Eph. 5:6 NAS; II Thess. 2:3 NKJ).

Well, are there any churches on the front lines doing battle with the "deceivers"? Fortunately yes, a resounding yes! There are churches, denominationally aligned, who are continuously and steadfastly persevering in the work of the Lord, with incredible blessing in numerical growth, as well as in spiritual and physical growth. They don't use any secret "mumbo-jumbo" or yard sales, Sunday morning breakfasts or bingo at any time ever. These churches do provide an environment for generic (non-doctrinaire) Bible study. This kind of encircling of the Holy Scriptures is the means by which God will bless and prepare those studying to be fitted for service in His vineyard.

That was the norm in the early Church and they were given the ability to speak out, to speak the Word of God with boldness (Acts 4:31).

Be Single-minded

The apostle Paul as a church planter and teacher tells the Corinthian church what every pastor must tell his congregants many times over: "For I am jealous over you with godly jealousy: for I have espoused you to one husband, that I may present you as a chaste virgin to Christ" (II Cor. 11:2 KJV). Believers are the Bride of Christ. Even though some interpret the verse to be directed more to the younger women of that time, it also relates to believers. The anticipated joy of a believer is fulfilled when they who were introduced to Christ acknowledge Him as their personal Savior and are presented to Him as chaste virgins to the glory of God and to the music of angelic choirs in Heaven.

Such a believer in the Lord Jesus Christ is someone whose primary aim in life is to be "well pleasing" to God (Phil. 4:18; Heb. 13:21). Paul explains how: "Study to shew thyself approved unto God, a workman that needeth not to be ashamed, rightly dividing [handling accurately] the word of truth" (II Tim. 2:15 KJV). The Ryrie Study Bible comments: " 'Handling accurately', i.e., correctly handling the Word of God, in both analysis and presentation—in contrast to the inane interpretations of false teachers" (p. 1826). "We are to avoid worldly and empty chatter, it leads to further ungodliness" (2 Tim. 2:16 NAV).

No successful businessman or businesswoman can be lethargic and irresponsible in their work. A laissez-faire apologist in the business, professional or academic world is not about to achieve any mind-boggling or spectacular success. The same principle holds true in the life of a believer.

Jesus achieved that kind of success. "But when the multitudes saw this [healing of paralytic], they were filled with awe, and glorified God, who had given such authority to men" (Matt. 9:8 NAS). Jesus' last words to the disciples before His ascension were "all power..." (Matt. 28:18ff. KJV). This power is freely dispensed to all believers (Acts 1:8). We, as believers, have the ability to succeed.

But just as sure as disobedience to God will limit your impact upon your family and neighbors, so your disobedience to satan will limit the impact satan, his fallen angels and his demon hosts can have in controlling your life. Instead you allow the Holy Spirit to control. Then the "Lord of Hosts," with Jehovah the captain of the armies, is at the front line.

Obey the Spirit

Experiencing the fulness of joy of a believer is predicated upon and circumscribed by a persevering faithfulness in obedience to the "still small voice" of the Holy Spirit. Even that great leader, Moses, was fallible, for his disobedience disbarred both him and Aaron from entering the Promised Land (Num. 20:12; Deut. 3:26-27). Moses even tried to shift the blame several times (Deut. 1:37; 4:21). All this notwithstanding, he did offer counsel (or was Moses sermonizing?) in his final remarks to the children of Israel.

I am sure there was sufficient blame to go around in that situation, but Moses was the "big man." Whether a million or more people are involved, as in Moses' case, or whether a congregation, a Sunday school class or your own family is involved, when you accept an appointment to serve, a heavy responsibility rests on your shoulders. God keeps accurate accounting in His Book and will hold you responsible for any miscarriage of or disrespect for the resources under your control.

There should be little or no margin for error with anyone appointed to leadership, especially in the Church, where God has provided a strict pattern that is to be respected. But if you put a hummingbird in the eagle's nest, then you will have problems.

Stay Alert

Notwithstanding your new birth, your new life in Christ, and the ministry of the Holy Spirit, Peter tells us "...Your adversary, the devil, prowls about like a roaring lion, seeking someone to devour" (1 Pet. 5:8 NAS). But again satan is seriously retarded, or has a failing knowledge of the reality of his defeat at Calvary, for satan does not take defeat easily. He will watch for any cracks in your armor and will take advantage of them if you allow him to do so. Satan will miss little, if anything, when you are working for God.

God's determinate wisdom and counsel is resolute throughout the totality of Scripture. No distortions in transmitting the message are to be countenanced. Beginning in Genesis and traceable in the New Testament, one finds the word "beware" or similar words like "take heed" which alert the reader and the hearer to "not believe every spirit [message], but test the spirits to see whether they are from God; because many false prophets have gone out into the world" (1 John 4:1 NAS).

Teaching the Kingdom of God

I am firmly convinced, and I say this without apology, that when the Holy Spirit initiates and accomplishes His exalted and glorified work in a person who is repentant and open to the leading of the Holy Spirit, that person will experience the new birth. By God's reckoning that person has become a new creation. This process is analogous to the Holy Spirit's work in the womb of the virgin Mary. This was a virgin creation, a new creation, with the entrance of the third Person of the Trinity, who gives "light...[and] understanding unto the simple" (Ps. 119:130 KJV). Indeed, "the kingdom of God is within you" (Luke 17:21b KJV).

Kingdom teaching for both the Jew and the believer seems to be something of a mystery. Presently the believer has more than that promised in Luke 17:21.

There Christ told the Pharisees that "the kingdom of God was in their midst," or among them, and not "within them." That was reserved for a future day and for believers, and the Pharisees did not believe.

That is what, I believe, Paul had as reference in Second Corinthians 5:17: "Therefore if anyone is in Christ, he is a new creation; old things have passed away; behold, all things have become new" (NKJ). The idiom or cast of the Greek words used, *kainos* for new and *ktisis* for creation, speak of freshness and newness and of original formation.

Therefore when God does something, we must believe it to be perfect, unblemished and virginal. It is that which God can then use for His glory.

When we as believers are raped by satan and sullied, we become useless, unprofitable and "unworthy of eternal life..." (Acts 13:46 NAS). Then there is no need to ask questions like, "Why am I not having answers to my prayers?" "Why do we not see a healing ministry in the Church?" "Why am I having so much trouble making ends meet?" Certainly God has not changed course. He has given us our instructional book, the Bible, which is the best, the most qualified, teacher.

Kingdom teaching was a practice of the early Church. In Acts and in the Epistles of Paul it can be found at least 22 times. The Kingdom of Heaven will be identifiable during the Millennium. Christ encouraged His disciples to preach Kingdom truth. The

Pharisees could not share in it since they could not believe. They "questioned" the Lord Jesus (Luke 17:20 NAS). None may question God. He gives freely after certain conditions are met. The Pharisees as a body did not understand that. A few individuals did and shared the blessings.

The Kingdom of God as a body of truth is vague to the person stained by worldly lusts spoken of in Titus 2:11-12. To the sincere believer, one who is obedient to the leading of the Holy Spirit, this truth invigorates and strengthens.

Luke draws our attention to this body of truth, the Kingdom of God, and it's significance to the inquiring heart is a theme of enormous spiritual consequence. This truth was apparently beyond the reach of the disciples. The context in which we find this teaching tells us the disciples were largely ineffective as hearers and doers. The Lord Jesus was coming to the end of His days upon earth and His concern was obviously for His followers to be alert. Throughout the final chapters of the Book of Luke He reminds of the need for forgiveness; the disciples see Him in the cleansing of the ten lepers; He discusses His return; then He admonishes them not to quit, He will come back from death, etc.

But the Kingdom was within each one of them who believed, and only then they would "desire to see one of the days of the Son of man, and ye shall not see it. And they shall say to you, See here; or, see there: go not after them, nor follow them" (Luke 17:22-23 KJV).

They not only did not hear and do, they were apparently unable to see. Paul says of Israel in Romans 11:25c: "That blindness in part is happened to Israel, *until* the fulness of the Gentiles be come in" (KJV).

Is there a parallel evident here for the Church of this day? I verily believe there is. Few in the waning days of the twentieth century or, more importantly, in the latter days of the 6000 years of man's history, are quite aware of the transient nature of the day and of the imminence of the coming of the Lord.

As in the times referred to in the text, so also the Lord is perfecting His saints at this time (2 Cor. 7:1 NAS).

When Matthew chronicled the genealogy of Christ, aiming his narrative at the Jewish audience, he used the term "Kingdom of Heaven" more often than any other writer. That is so for obvious reasons. The Kingdom of Heaven, in context, has reference to another time, and exegetical license suggests application to Israel—a time of post-tribulation fulfillment. Matthew makes mention of the trial, the Crucifixion, the Resurrection and the return of Christ to earth to address the importance of the "Great Commission": Go! Teach! Baptize!

The Need to Speak and Teach

"Clear and present danger" is a phrase used in a court of law. This phrase represents a standard used to determine when one's right to speak may be curtailed, etc. Satan is dedicated to curtailing your right to speak. But we too have first amendment rights as believers. "Cry loudly, do not hold back; raise your voice like a trumpet, and declare to My people their transgression..." (Is. 58:1 NAS). It is a command, not an option. Satan has been eminently successful in curtailing Christians' speech. Believers do present a clear and present danger to his avowed program, for the believer is satan's archenemy.

You as a believer need to know that you must be effective as an advocate of the Lord Jesus. You and I must adversely and conclusively stem the perversities and lies of satan. The conduct of and success of the believer in his or her ongoing conflict with satan is energized by the words of the prophet Zechariah: " 'Not by might nor by power, but by My Spirit,' says the LORD of hosts" (Zech. 4:6 NAS). The reference "Lord of hosts" can be read as "Jehovah of the armies." The Lord will not hold back any of His battle-ready troops when He sees His children in present and certain danger. Nothing is more important to our Heavenly Father than His children, for His only begotten Son gave His life for them and Christ Jesus is in daily intercession before the throne on their behalf.

Our children need to learn from God's Word, our testimony and thus by our teaching them the "pattern" (2 Tim. 2:2). In this context children include all ages: from 7 and younger to 70 and older. To be called young is not an impediment or stigma. Teaching is not a dirty word. But the presence of or lack of teaching is the determinant that influences your behavioral development throughout your life. There is an abundance of teaching today. The state-controlled schools teach the care and benevolence of the welfare state. What television teaches has little permanent value. Unfortunately the programming in sitcoms and other shows have a compelling proclivity for showing spectacularly sexual and brutal conduct. The drug culture and the ever-expanding display of deviate sexual lifestyles all takes place in our living rooms on the TV screens.

If children will be children, (and they will be children), it must follow that parenting be the priority of the day; that is, if we want to bring our families and our country back to a gentler, more caring society.

It is small wonder that the Church is seen to be in a state of quarantine when you hear the voices coming from the pulpits around the country. Where is the missionary emphasis? Or, more to the point, where is the local church that speaks with the eloquence of a C.H. Spurgeon, a John Wesley or a Dwight L. Moody? These men and other spiritual, Bible-preaching men of earlier times addressed these issues with fervor and called for decisions concerning salvation and commitment to fulltime service.

The top priority of the Church should be involving its congregants, and especially the youth, in generic Bible study that founds and contributes to doctrinally sound and biblically energized, Bible-centered preaching. That kind of ministry excites young people. They start thinking seriously about their commitment to the call of Christ. "Do you not say, 'There are yet four months, and then comes the harvest'? Behold, I say to you, lift up your eyes, and look on the fields, that they are white for harvest" (John 4:35 NAS). Yes, there are wages to be earned and fruit to be gathered (see verse 36).

The Need to Preach

There appears to be more passivity in the Church today than ever before. The apostle Peter might not have had the anemic hearers of our day, but in the opening words of his sermons he admonishes his hearers to "give heed to my words" before proceeding to quote the prophetic Scriptures.

In Acts chapters 2 and 3, Peter preaches twice in rapid succession. Peter had a crowd. The lame beggar with whom the multitudes were familiar had received his healing, and much joy resulted from this man being healed. Is there a lesson here for the Church? I believe so. Peter did not speak to empty pews, as is often the case today. He had a crowd. The crowd believed something more was about to happen. But he begins his message on a negative premise. Peter calls attention to their rejection or denial of the "Holy One," albeit they did it in ignorance. Peter continues to the point where he admonishes them to "repent therefore and be converted, that your sins may be blotted out, so that times of refreshing may come from the presence of the Lord" (Acts 3:19 NKJ).

One of the shortcomings in today's Church is our inability to attract people to listen to the message of the gospel. No doubt the questions outnumber the answers, but there is really only one answer to the empty pew syndrome. That answer comes across loud and clear: "Preach the Word...." The Holy Spirit will bless the Word that is preached and will add daily those who are being saved.

"Preach the Word then tell the world." That is precisely what the world does. Consider the business sector. If merchants ceased communicating to the world weekly, even daily, their doors would close for want of business. "For the children of this world are in their generation wiser than the children of light" (Luke 16:8b KJV). We are children of light. The Father has all the riches of the world and is waiting to share this wealth with His children. But because we do not believe or follow the pattern which pleases Him, the blessings are not forthcoming. "Preach the word; be instant in season, out of season; reprove, rebuke, exhort with all longsuffering and doctrine" (II Tim. 4:2 KJV).

"Preach the Word," Paul says. "Be instant...." The nuances in the original Greek suggest "stand upon" and "assault." Thus it must ever be one of assault against the forces of evil.

Paul said further that if he should be unable to stand, God could, for His "strength is made perfect in weakness" (II Cor. 12:9 KJV). In Ephesians chapter 6 he talks of needing the whole armor of God in order to stand in the evil day (v. 13). The armor is required for both the person in the pew and the leader in the Church. "Every kingdom divided against itself is brought to desolation; and every city or house divided against itself shall not stand" (Matt. 12:25b KJV).

I, for one, am ready to bring pressure upon the Church leaders, imploring, even insisting upon more Biblical engagement. Someone has said, in jest no doubt, that the seminaries, (or are they cemeteries?) have been producing a sleepy clique of pulpiteers prepared each Sunday to "preach" a 15 minute or, if one is lucky, a 20 minute sermonette.

To be sure, this phenomenon does not belong to the twentieth century alone. The prophets Isaiah and Nahum chided their leaders in their day: "His watchmen are blind, all of them know nothing. All of them are dumb dogs unable to bark, dreamers lying down, who love to slumber" (Is. 56:10 NAS); "Your shepherds are sleeping, O king of Assyria; your nobles are lying down. Your people are scattered on the mountains, and there is no one to regather them" (Nah. 3:18 NAS).

To me the prevailing mood in the Church today seems to be, "Let's not make waves and everything will turn out all right." That was neither the attitude nor the conviction of the early New Testament Church. (See Acts 17:6, 11-13.) Here we find the apostle Paul at Thessalonica doing what he did so well and the reaction was, "These men who have upset the world have come here also" (v. 6), and why, you ask? "For they received the word [of God] with great eagerness, examining the Scriptures daily..." (v. 11b NAS).

2

After the Pattern

"After the pattern" is a phrase iterated and reiterated time and again. "According to all that I am going to show you, as the pattern of the tabernacle and the pattern of all its furniture, just so you shall construct it" (Ex. 25:9 NAS). "Now this was the workmanship of the lampstand, hammered work of gold... according to the pattern..." (Num. 8:4 NAS). "Son of man, describe the temple to the house of Israel, that they may be ashamed of their iniquities; and let them measure the pattern" (Ezek. 43:10 NKJ). In Ezekiel's time there was compelling evidence that the pattern was not closely followed, if followed at all. So there was shame: "And if they are ashamed of all they have done, make known to them...write it in their sight, so that they may observe....This is the law of the house..." (Ezek. 43:11-12 NAS).

In these Old Testament verses God is showing His perfection and His exactitude concerning His dwelling place. God is no less uncaring when it comes to the

New Testament Church, as recorded in the Book of the Acts of the Apostles and in the messages to the churches from Paul and John.

"And day by day continuing with one mind in the temple, and breaking bread...praising God, and having favor with all the people. And the Lord was adding to their number day by day those who were being saved" (Acts 2:46-47 NAS).

The Pattern of the Tabernacle

God appropriately set before Moses the ultimatum that must be respected. God has a workable pattern for the building of His tabernacle, for the instruments used in the course of worship, for the altar and for other items (Ex. 25:9, 40; Josh. 22:28; 1 Chron. 28:11).

When the reader notes the significance of the things mentioned, he or she sees a beautiful and majestic analogy. Each item is representative of the believer in Christ. The believer is the tabernacle of the Holy Spirit. He has blessed each one of us with all the necessary instruments to validate the assignment to which we have been called. The altar for Israel in former times represented the benefits from the sacrifices; to the believer the altar signifies God's benefits because of the sacrificial death of Christ as well as a place to meet God.

Throughout Israel's history, beginning with the commandments in Exodus chapter 20, God tells Moses that He is a jealous God and will visit the "iniquity of the fathers [not the mothers] on the children, on the third and the fourth generations of those who hate Me" (Ex. 20:5 NAS). Yes, there is a love/hate relationship with God. There is no gray area. You are either one of His children, or not one of His children. The determining factor with Israel was their "whoring" with Molech (Lev. 20:5 KJV). In this case both men and women as well as their families were "cut off." This judgment reaches far beyond the purely spiritual dogmatism of the Mosaic law or teaching. This teaching, if submitted to, carries great and precious promises and unbridled success.

Concerning God's command to follow the pattern, do not overlook the inference to perfection and exactitude. For example, it is interesting to note the workmanship necessary for the lampstand. The lampstand was to be a "hammered work of gold" (Num. 8:4 NAS). "You are the light of the world. A city set on a hill cannot be hidden" (Matt. 5:14 NAS). You are a "mountain." The mountain speaks of elevation and openness, thus the light cannot be easily hidden from view and is fair game for the enemy. Using the metaphor of light, you may be encouraged to know that God so views each one of us who are His children. The world is watching us. Let it not be said of us that we will be shamed for slovenliness. God told Ezekiel that Israel would sin and "be ashamed of their iniquities…" (Ezek. 43:10 NAS).

We are God's lampstand of hammered gold. Hammered gold is both expensive and beautiful. Sometimes we are "hammered" or "buffeted" (I Pet. 2:20

KJV) with reason; we may be unspiritual. In any case, He desires the lampstand to be a thing of beauty, for it is what holds the light. Moreover, as the lampstand is of elegant gold, so also is "the elegance of your faith, being much more precious than gold that perishes, though it is tested by fire" (I Pet. 1:7 NKJ). You who believe are more precious than gold which perishes, because your faith announces to the world who you are and to whom you belong. God made the world for you for God so loved the world. Satan knows that and is more angry with you when your heart is filled with praise for that glory God shares with you in your willing and obedient service.

The Pattern in the Prodigal Son

Most of us have heard at one time or another the story of the prodigal son. In this story the name of the father is not given, no doubt because the parable was intended to show the discontent which can so easily erupt in a family and among kinfolk. Unfortunately, this untoward conduct has extended in a wider circle of society.

In the storyline, as recorded in Luke chapter 15, one of two sons expresses his dissatisfaction to his father. He requests his father to give him his inheritance because he wanted to "split" from the family and go his own way.

Interestingly enough the father fulfills his son's request and measures out the portion of the bequest that rightfully belonged to the son. There was no rebuttal or refusal on the part of the father.

The story has a deeper meaning, however. In the beginning verses of chapter 15 we find a thought-inspiring reference to two other "lost" entities, one sheep (v. 4) and one coin (v. 8). One sheep, one coin and now one son is lost.

The sheep and the coin were diligently sought for, and were found. The son was not. He had made a moral choice; the sheep and the coin were incapable of making that kind of choice. Others had the responsibility for finding the sheep and the coin. The son had a personal responsibility for finding his way out of his dilemma.

The story continues with the son spending all his inheritance. The phrase "spent all" in the Greek idiom points to his living ruinously. In other words, he was wasteful and profligate. There is pleasure in sin, but those pleasures are passing (see Hebrews 11:25 NAS).

As the father was in the storyline, so also is our Heavenly Father. He never forces anyone to be born again. He never forces anyone to remain in the family against that person's will. He allows you to make personal and moral choices to your own hurt. If without repentance and remorse, the judgment of God awaits His divine command that expedites the penalty with authority.

The possibility of penalty was facing the son. He had squandered his capital, wasted his time foolishly and he was getting hungrier by the hour. We are told that he "came to himself." Such **persuasion of** retrospect dictates a course of action. A sobering soliloquy ensues about the father and home. The son was reasoning objectively, probably for the first time in his short life. "I will arise...and will say...I have sinned...[then] he arose, and came to his father."

Ah, yes. What was the father's response? The father saw his son "a great way off" and "had compassion, and ran, and fell on his neck, and kissed him." "And they began to be merry."

There is more to the story, and I'd remind the reader of its prophetic overtones. This narrative shows Jesus treating the commonplace with sublime truth. His message calls the disciples and Israel to bear witness to the truth of the parable. "He that hath ears to hear, let him hear" is an oft-quoted phrase throughout all the Scriptures.

There is more than just the "prophetic overtones" or "prophetic facet." In fact, several additional facets might apply. The Church facet and the believer facet are also found in the storyline. Like a gorgeous diamond with its many facets is the Word of God. That is what provides the zealous student of the Word with such consummate pleasure.

In the parable the son had to verify his identity, even among the pigs. For a Jew, tending pigs was the worst, the most degrading, kind of employment. Not until the son admitted to himself the extent of his degradation did he find making his decision to be conscionable.

He was actually living with the pigs, wallowing in their mire. But he didn't partake of their food, their drink, their cocaine or their wine. He said to himself, "I'm going home. This is no way to live."

The storyline of the prodigal son quite vividly mirrors the actions and activities of Israel throughout her history.

For example, when in Egypt during the famine and under the charge of Joseph, the vice-regent under the pharaoh, Israel's needs were adequately met in the fertile region of Goshen. In the midst of the famine, as severe as it was, Joseph called on Israel to give not 10 percent, but 20 percent to the pharaoh. While in Egypt and despite recession, depression, famine, etc., the people of Israel knew no lack. What a blessed demonstration of God's provision in times of economic despair. To expedite their removal from Egypt, they were requested to take articles of silver, of gold and of clothing (Ex. 12:35-36). Six hundred thousand men on foot, aside from children (Ex. 12:37 NAS), were never without divine supervision and direction. When it was time to leave Egypt and journey to the Promised Land, the presence of God accompanied them, meeting their needs for each day. His presence was visible in the cloud by day and the pillar of fire by night. But the people exercised their freedom by complaints, bitterness and ingratitude.

Did Israel ever realize their sin and rebellion against God? They hadn't in the times of the patriarchs, the kings or the prophets, or even when God sent His only Son into the world, one of Israel's own, He who said, "I am the root and the offspring of

David..." (Rev. 22:16b KJV). Instead they crucified the "Lord of glory" (1 Cor. 2:8 NAS); that "blindness...happened to Israel..." (Rom. 11:25 KJV).

Paul told that fact about Israel to the church at Rome. The Church today, in its chameleon-like lifestyle, needs to be confronted head-on with the ultimate truth: God still has a pattern for His Church, as clearly defined as it was to the early Church.

But for Israel's disobedience, the Jews' history would have differed. Instead, they endured unmerciful suffering with the pogroms of Russia and the Holocaust of Germany. Presently they still endure hostilities, bloodshed and epidemic insanity of political leaders. But Almighty God alone knows the cause of the problem, and He alone will ultimately be called up to say "enough is enough."

Israel fell because they moved out of the range of God's control. Thus the sin-contaminated, pathological derangement of a large part of the world's society fell upon them.

Why does the Church need to know of Israel's history? It follows logically that the Church, you and me, must be on guard also. "Now these things happened to them as an example, and they were written for our instruction, upon whom the ends of the ages have come" (1 Cor. 10:11 NAS).

You may visit the pigs, you may even live like they do. But you dare not wallow in the mire with them. Guard your pearls, for pigs are not interested in pearls

(Matt. 7:6). All they want is food, even garbage. When you are among pigs you won't be interested in heavenly manna.

Are you frantic and anxious about unanswered prayer? Leave the pigpen and go back to your Father's house. You will be received with joy and be restored. You, as a believer, *must* verify your identity. The prodigal son was unsure of his father's willingness to re-instate him. He need not have been. Accordingly, we should not question God's ability to fulfill our prayer requests. (Too often we support our problems.) His reach goes far beyond our ability to touch or grasp.

Our knowledge diligently supports what we know! It finds little that is harmonious with the known Scripture, with the Holy Spirit and with His poignant appeal. Human logic tends to be fractious and divisive. But the appeal of the Holy Spirit is to urgently fulfill, without interruption, the desires of our Heavenly Father. "For God so loved the world...." We must believe beyond knowledge.

3

Paul: A Man of Destiny

The apostle Paul, otherwise known as Rav Sha-ul, had no peers. He was penultimate in rabbinical knowledge and practices. This man, though a Jew, was proud of his Roman citizenship and of his Greek education which gave him high marks in the academic and collegial society with which he was identified. But this famous Rabbi Sha-ul met a Man one day on the way to Damascus. This Man had the Light; He was the Light. The account of this meeting in the Book of Acts does not state the size of the Light, whether it was large or small. Nonetheless, the Light was of sufficient size and importance to "get his attention" and cause this Rabbi to start asking questions. This Rabbi asks a profound question. "Was this mere happenstance?" No, for God's grace has no restraints.

His Conversion

The first mention of Saul is found in Acts 7:58 through Acts 8:4 where, following the account of

Stephen's stoning, is described the "great persecution [that] arose against the church in Jerusalem...ravaging the church, entering house after house; and dragging off men and women, he would put them in prison" (Acts 8:1-3 NAS). Notwithstanding the persecution and their being "scattered [they] went about preaching the Word" (Acts 8:4 NAS).

Thus, in chapters 8 through 13 of Acts, Saul, whose name by transliteration means "asked for," (Unger, Bible Dict. p. 973) had stature in that society. Then comes a name change to Paul, from the Greek form of Paulos which means "little" (Unger, Bible Dict. p. 831).

Paul was "asked for" by God, whereupon the Holy Spirit took over and prompted the answer, "Who art Thou, Lord?" (Acts 9:5 NAS). His response did not come from his rabbinic training. Even in our day no orthodox Jew will so much as pronounce the name of God for fear of desecrating that Name. So the response of Saul was of supernatural origin.

The Holy Spirit will not violate any of your firm opinions until after He has secured you for membership in God's family. The Church was born, or brought into existence, before Paul's conversion. Paul could be assimilated into the Church by only one way. He had to hear God's voice. Then by praying and by obeying His command, Paul was led into the presence of another who could give him the information that God said: "...he is a chosen instrument of Mine, to bear My name before the Gentiles and kings and the sons of Israel" (Acts 9:15 NAS).

That is the pattern God presents to all who would be His children. The best advice to the would-be soul winner or witness is #1. Secure the person's attention by whatever means. The means might not be a light flashing from heaven. God the Holy Spirit is not limited to that means alone. But He will use appropriate and significant things, be it a rod as in Moses' time or stones as in David's encounter. Be assured that God has more attention-getters than you might ever suspect. In every encounter you have in witnessing, you first secure their attention before articulating or expressing distinctly the terms under discussion. In Saul's experience, as in every witnessing encounter, conviction is to be expected. Attention, articulation, conviction; these three will invariably lead to an expressed desire to learn more. There may even be another apostle Paul ready to do today what was done by the early Church: They "...turned the world upside down..." (Acts 17:6 KJV).

Paul refers to the incident thus: "And last of all he was seen of one also, as of one born out of due time" (I Cor. 15:8 KJV). He seems to imply that he did not qualify himself as one of the twelve apostles because the twelve were personal eyewitnesses of His majesty. (See Second Peter 1:16.) But God had "asked for" this man to fulfill a divinely ordained ministry in the Church during its immature and developing stages. The Church of today, as well as through its last 1900 years, is a benefactor of and a debtor to this great apostle for the unwavering authority he ascribed to the Word of God.

Whatever anyone might say to the contrary, Paul refers to himself as least among the apostles (1 Cor. 15:9; Eph. 3:8). At the same time, however, he does say what may sound contradictory to some people: "Brethren, be followers together of me, and mark them which walk so as ye have us for an ensample [example]" (Phil. 3:17 KJV). The word *tupos* is translated as "example." Paul used this word 12 times in his writings. The translators usually rendered the word as "pattern." For example, the Thessalonians became models, or a pattern, to the believers in Macedonia and Achaia (1 Thess. 1:6-7 ASRV).

Paul is a pattern for believers, a spiritual virgin whose concern was the birthing of more believers.

His Testimony

Paul's dedication to his calling infuriated some. Paul was seized in Jerusalem. He had subsequent appearances before the council at Jerusalem. He was moved to Caesarea for his appearances before Felix, Festus and Agrippa. Then Paul was sent to Rome as a prisoner, for reasons almost too insignificant to mention. Paul, being an evangelist/preacher, was the source of intense hostility. The Jews' fanaticism, religious in concept, prevailed; it was a "zeal for God, but not in accordance with knowledge" (Rom. 10:2 NAS).

The apostle Paul is careful to note some details of his own background as he stood before the judgment seat of the various authorities of the Empire. He kept to the truth and to his testimony. He made some eye-opening comments which had to be a source of considerable astonishment to his hearers. For that reason and others he was moved from one praetorium to another, finally being sent to Rome for his final adjudication.

The beloved apostle unabashedly and literally tells all. "...I went about preaching...I testify to you this day, that I am *innocent* of the blood of all men. For I did not shrink from declaring to you the whole purpose of God" (Acts 20:25-27 NAS). When before the council, "Paul, looking intently at the Council, said, 'Brethren, I have lived my life with a perfectly good conscience before God up to this day'" (Acts 23:1 NAS). And when Paul was before Felix he said, "...I cheerfully make my defense [*apologia*, Gr.]" (Acts 24:10 NAS). Cheerfully? At a time like that Paul could be cheerful?

The capstone to Paul's testimony leaves no doubt as to the stature of this great man of God, and in truth he was just that. Paul's conduct and activity as a religionist, incidentally, was fully authorized by the puristic hyper-orthodoxy of that day. But that changed, for he met a Man on the way to Damascus, a bright Light.... That Light was from Heaven. He heard a voice, a call with a question, "Why?" "Saul, Saul, why are you persecuting Me?" (Acts 9:4 NAS). That voice, the voice of authority, was enough to summon the apostle's attention. That voice is calling today, but modern mankind is preoccupied with the myriad voices screaming for attention. Thus we are deprived of blessings from on high.

Later on in Paul's ministry he confesses his faulted behavior. His perspective had been mis-directed...for "he thought." Extra-biblical thought is painfully current today. So much of what proceeds out of the mouths of Christians mirrors Paul's words: "So then, I *thought to myself* that I had to do many things hostile to the name of Jesus of Nazareth. And this is just what I did in Jerusalem; not only did I lock up many of the saints in prisons, having received authority from the chief priests, but also when they were being put to death I cast my vote against them" (Acts 26:9-10 NAS).

The Spirit of the Lord, in an earlier day, spoke to the prophet Ezekiel: "Say, 'Thus says the LORD, "So you *think*, house of Israel, for I know your thoughts," ' " (Ezek. 11:5 NAS).

No, it is not wrong to think. All of us do our share of thinking. But, as Paul states in his own case, our thoughts are not always consistent with the thoughts of the Holy Spirit, or with the mind of Christ: "Let this mind be in you, which was also in Christ Jesus" (Phil. 2:5 KJV). More often then any of us will admit, we are intractable hedonists. The end result is disaster.

His Character

We stated earlier that Paul's name means "little." The incidents in Paul's life indicate everything but little. He was a spiritual giant.

The apostle Paul was not insensate. His concern for people was beautifully expressed, with emotional anxiety, for his "kinsmen according to the flesh" and for mankind in totality (Rom. 9:3ff. KJV).

This ardent missionary, this man of force and action, had no need for pomp and circumstance or for security, quite unlike our present day TV ministers. Those everyday sins of pride and self-gratification are absent from his ministry and writings. With characteristic delicacy he approaches the people on his various journeys and in his writings, without an apostolic claim. He preaches fearlessly, addressing the center of the Empire: Rome. In reading the account by Luke, Paul's amanuensis, in the Book of the Acts of the Apostles, we can easily surmise that "all roads lead to Rome." "To all who are beloved of God in Rome, called as saints..." (Rom. 1:7 NAS). That is where he did finish his missionary/ministry activity. The apostle's goal was to *finish* the course. "But I do not consider my life of any account as dear to myself, in order that I may finish *my* course, and the ministry which I received from the Lord Jesus, to testify solemnly of the gospel of the grace of God" (Acts 20:24 NAS; see also Second Timothy 4:7-8). Failure to finish is tantamount to rejecting the voice of authority.

His Call

Paul was the bearer of the flame. But he was tethered, he had a "mooring rope" to which he was attached, for he was "called ...as an apostle, set apart for the gospel of God" (Rom. 1:1 NAS).

Our present day evangelists and pastors have, on their own initiative, lengthened their cords to where not only their message, but also their outreach, is out of bounds. Thus the Church has become little more than a social club, a place where one goes for aerobics, book reviews and any other nonsensical venture. The Church, which was to be set aside for the "gospel of God," is being used for serving meals in order to "meet the budget."

The gospel of God thrives upon teaching the Word. That is precisely what the apostles did in the early Church. Salvation was *the* word, and is so stated by Peter in Acts 4:12: "And there is salvation in no one else; for there is no other name under heaven that has been given among men, by which we *must* be saved" (NAS).

Paul was a man of destiny. A predetermined course was set in motion for him on that Damascus road. He was not without some foreknowledge of the inevitable in the fulfilling of his ministry. "He must suffer for My name's sake" (Acts 9:16b NAS). "...The Holy Spirit solemnly testifies to me in every city, saying that bonds and afflictions await me" (Acts 20:23 NAS). (See also Acts 21:4, 11, 13; Second Corinthians 6:4f.; 11:23-27.) To the Thessalonians Paul writes, "...we have been destined for this" (1 Thess. 3:3 NAS). Herein is displayed the resistless power, that motivation, that Paul had, despite the foreordained future.

We like sometimes to juxtapose our present day "men of the cloth" with the apostle Paul. Paul was intimidated by no one in the political precincts, in the religious community where he played a significant role or in the groves of academe where he sat at the feet of Gamaliel, one "in reputation among all the people" (Acts 5:34 KJV). In Acts 22:3 Gamaliel was the preceptor of the apostle Paul. Anyone having Gamaliel as friend and mentor could countervail among the empirical politics of that day (see Acts 5:34-39).

History records Paul as a man of distinction. His writings are remembered and quoted far and wide to the benefit of all who will hear.

His Environment

This question might be asked: "Was Paul as a Christian, or for that matter, were any Christians, welcome at that time when authoritarian Rome wielded sovereignty?" The Roman procurators were heavy-handed and stood ready to maintain law and order, to preside over judicial affairs, etc.

The appointment of these officials was on the line at all times, for they were closely monitored. The hierarchy of the Roman Empire was diligently suspicious of the Jews and of potential insurrection.

Thus throughout history, when the Jew fell under the heel of a conqueror, tension always materialized. It was in this environment that Paul and his fellow Christians were carefully policed. Freedom was always within protected parameters. This oppressive governance eventually manifested signs of political deterioration and weakness, considerably around the third and fourth centuries, AD.

We must remember too that Paul was disliked by the religious community ever since he "converted" to Christ the Messiah and thereby vacated his rabbinate vows and his subservience to the authorities of the synagogue and the government. Moreover, Paul spoke out against the evils they condoned if not in fact promulgated. These burdensome laws required a voice of protest. The synagogue's restraints conflicted with the message of Christ and required a strong and believable or credible outcry. Paul's was a lone voice, a "voice of one crying in the wilderness" (Isa. 40:3; John 1:23 NKJ).

His Ministry

A century ago it was the custom for preachers to exercise great influence in political matters. In fact, the minister once exercised most of the functions that lately have been appropriated by the print columnists, by the television and radio commentators, by the editorial writer and the magazine essayist. The minister is "relegated" to "spiritual" matters. Hogwash!

Paul, John and James spoke to the Church and the Church was looked upon as the microcosm of society. The pulpit had a message for society and its ills. Anyone who is alert today and who observes objectively must be troubled, if not angry. It is most certainly the function of the minister to speak against iniquity in any form in order to protect the interests of his congregants.

It will be increasingly urgent for ministers of the gospel to speak out on political matters, for the political power structures seek to control our destiny. These operatives are alien to the gospel of Jesus Christ and so must be exposed. As the apostle Paul told the church at Thessalonica, "...we have been destined for this" (1 Thess. 3:3 NAS).

Yes! The apostle Paul was a man of destiny who, though dead, yet speaks.

Is this kind of ministry accomplished without dangerous consequences? No; there is a price to pay. James was murdered, Peter was crucified, Paul was beheaded in Rome and John was banished to the Isle of Patmos. In fact, the history of the Church abounds with the bloodshed of the warriors of the cross.

Something has gone out of control in today's Church leadership. However, according to the current Spirit-filled cadre of Bible scholars, they are hearing "the sound of a going in the tops of the mulberry trees..." (II Sam. 5:24; I Chron. 14:15 KJV).

Observing the events unfolding worldwide, these scholars see a revived Roman Empire similar to the one Paul dealt with during his ministry. There is the possibility that the Church will again be subjected to fierceness, despair, martyrdom and woes.

History repeats itself; it has a pattern. Bacon said that history makes a wise man (Essays and the New Atlantis, 108). We would do well to take serious heed.

The Need for Paul's Pattern Today

The Church today suffers an affliction called cyanosis which, according to Webster's Dictionary, is "a condition in which the surface of the body becomes blue because of insufficient aeration of the blood...." The Church struggles with an apathetic interest in Bible study, anemic members, low church attendance, high dilution of membership from the rolls, withholding of tithes or the misuse of the same in supporting "one verse Charlies" with 12 or 15 minute sermonettes.

Who in our day preaches from all the Scriptures, in a book by book, verse by verse, line by line generic study format? The Church must demand from its pastors a compelling involvement in preaching the Word. The prophet Isaiah spoke: "Cry aloud, spare not, lift up thy voice like a trumpet, and *show* my people their transgression, and the house of Jacob their sins" (58:1 KJV). Today the issue of sin is counteractive and nonessential to the gospel agenda.

The "men of the cloth" who refuse to take a stand will be friends with "new" methods of religious expression, (e.g. Muslim, reincarnation, New Age, etc.). All of those are of satan, meticulously orchestrated by the master schemer of destruction (John 10:10). Do you think most "Christians" can tell the difference? No! They'll think that what they are hearing is quite nice and no doubt "cool." The present profusion and proliferation of ideologies that have religious-sounding overtones put unthinking Christian people in harm's way. "To the law and to the testimony! If they do not speak according to this word, it is because there is no light in them" (Isa. 8:20 NKJ). Any other preaching short of that strong statement is preaching with subversive intent. The words of Christ need no further interpretative comment. "He who is not with Me is against Me..." (Matt. 12:30; Luke 11:23 NKJ).

How can anyone improve on that? But the radical, liberal humanist will use whatever adds to his agenda, "for there are many unruly and vain talkers and deceivers, specially they of the circumcision [religionist]: whose mouths must be stopped, who subvert whole houses, teaching things which they ought not for filthy lucre's sake" (Titus 1:10-11 KJV). The church of my own early days is a treasured remembrance of a people filled with faith because they heard the Word, believed the Word and obeyed the Word. A return to the practices of those by-gone days would be well for the believers of this day.

4

"Born Again"

Nicodemus' Question

The apostle Paul was a conscript; Nicodemus was a suspect. The apostle's call was one of compulsion; Nicodemus' call elicited concern and confusion. Like so many people whom we meet, Nicodemus had questions. With his academic and political mindset he had concerns. These concerns were momentarily perplexing and imperceptible to him. "I need answers and I will listen. So, what does it mean to be born again, or more properly, to 'be born from above'?"

Immediately we have the answer stated simply, but circumscribed as a priority without options. The answer the Lord Jesus gave was unequivocal, candid and clearly directed (John 3:3, 7). It is fundamental; it is a requirement ordained of God. Any deviation from or violation of this divine principle incurs God's anger. One must recognize too that the disciples were present and no doubt had questions also. Although

Nicodemus was the point man in this encounter, the disciples who were present were introduced to this initial step in their training. Jesus' answer was the first step in developing a faculty relationship with the disciples.

But who was Nicodemus? An eminent and respected member of the Sanhedrin, some say he was Nicodemus Ben Gorion, a brother of Josephus the historian, also one of the richest men in Jerusalem. He was a man of dignified importance. (See Unger's Bible Dictionary.) But station in society doesn't matter; "unless one is born again, he cannot see the kingdom of God" (John 3:3 NAS).

Now the question. "How...?" Jesus answers Nicodemus (please observe the principle of natural law), "That which is born of the flesh is flesh; that is natural and with that you are familiar. But Nicodemus, I am speaking to you of something that is beyond your ability to comprehend fully. Yet just as the wind blows, you feel it and hear it, so also when a person is born from above, you feel it because you have heard the voice" (see John 3:5-8).

Only five words, "You must be born again," but the idiom of the original suggests a "'blast of power'...'the Spirit,' the 'wind,' 'current of air,' 'breath'." We remain unable to describe the influence of the Holy Spirit and the power of the Word to effect the miracle of the new birth. Those five words, "You must be born again," were a blast of power, the like of which had not been previously known or experienced, ever, in all of Israel's history. It was indeed a new thing. Isaiah 43:19 speaks of a "new thing." "Behold, I will do a *new* thing; now it shall spring forth; shall ye not know it? I will even make a way in the wilderness, and rivers in the desert" (KJV).

Those five words may be repugnant, distasteful and unpalatable to the modern day seminarian with liberal, humanist, theological preferences. Notwithstanding, modern ecumenism would like to be the conciliar element in society at large and that element might be tolerated were it not for their implausible position papers in the print and telecommunications media.

But to receive Christ Jesus as one's personal Savior is a blessing replete with rewards throughout all eternity. It's an ongoing experience: enduring and immortal. Shakespeare reportedly said, "I have immortal longings in me" (Shakespeare as quoted in Webster 2nd Ed. Dictionary, G & C Merriam Co., 1934, p. 1246). Much more so must the believer. Those longings are satisfied by the blessing of salvation, which finds its ultimate sufficiency in the New Testament. So the believer is delivered from the power and dominion of sin. Sin is the reason man must be born again.

Adam's Sin

God will not look favorably on anyone who will not heed His commandments. Adam and his wife quickly learned that sin cannot be concealed. Adam's sin was fully realized. Their eyes were opened. They went into hiding, but the sinner who commits sin against God's revealed will very soon finds there is no hiding place.

Adam is a negative as well as positive model for mankind for all time. He had a gracious Father who provided for his every present need and all his future needs. The promise to Adam was inviolate, permanent, sacred and with but one restriction. The message to Adam was clearly stated, the restriction was not ambiguous, and Adam fully understood it.

At a later period in time an angel visited a virgin maiden named Mary. God needed a willing and obedient person to fulfill His paternal desire and plan for mankind. So the angel announced to her that God was about to enter into her life to perform that miracle. In the virgin Mary as in Adam, God would bring to fruition the most astonishing, miraculous and crowning effort on His part, never again to be replicated, to prove once more His love and concern for His creation. That entity is called man, made in the image of God and considered "the apple of his eye" (Deut. 32:10 KJV).

Because the first Adam disobeyed the word of God and thus sinned, his seed was and is forever under the curse laid upon him. His sinning opened the way for "the serpent of old who is called the devil and Satan..." (Rev. 12:9 NAS), and it was he who "deceived Eve by his craftiness..." (II Cor. 11:3 NKJ).

Speech

Do you suppose the serpent spoke to Eve in deceiving her to taste of the fruit? Although the Bible does not state categorically that satan ordered Eve to eat of the tree, he did converse with her, questioning what God had said and whether or not God really meant what He said.

Some have advanced the supposition that the serpent might have had the ability to speak, that the animal might have had a voice box and the organs necessary for speech, but lost this ability in the curse pronounced upon it. But speech is shared in our day with no other living thing in the whole of God's creation. Man is intrinsically gifted for communication. His is intelligible and intelligent speech. Speech is the inalienable endowment of heavenly grace.

With this enduement called speech, it follows that God expects, even demands of, each of His children to obey His command. "Go...Tell...." Speech is the inalienable privilege reserved for mankind alone. However, the student of Scripture is readily reminded that man misuses his tongue to his own detriment and to the hurt of others. In the Books of Job, Psalms, Proverbs, Isaiah and in the whole of the New Testament, especially in the Book of James, there is instance after instance of scurrilous talk and damaging speech, but a shocking lack of scrupulous and caring conversation, speech that is beneficial for others.

Speech is the missing component in the Church today. The Church is the silent partner. All about us, in our great metropolitan areas to our small towns, all close their eyes to mayhem, murders, rapes, robberies and drug peddling. Even more sobering is the disintegration of the family, which is a vital component in our society if we are to survive. The Church is the silent partner, mesmerized by Hollywood and the media.

The two most valuable sense organs we have, the ears and eyes, have been rendered ineffective with satanic subtlety. The Church is becoming less interested, as a group, in Bible study. Consequently, the Church is less familiar with its textbook, the Bible. Sin in all its complexities is becoming more defiant, more blatantly uncontrollable, so, "Why do we sit here until we die?" (2 Kings 7:3 NAS). The Lord's command to go and teach has not been rescinded.

Obedience Is the Answer

Adam was the primal seed in God's creative process and instantaneous primogeniture, he being the firstborn of all mankind. On his shoulders, therefore, fell the responsibility of supremacy and leadership over all his progeny. Adam was the man to whom God gave specific instructions, which were not believed. Thus both Adam and his wife were disbarred from the Garden. Adam sinned in unbelief, and he was the designated head of that family. As always, the husband and father of the family bears the stigma of the sin of he and his family. He will be held culpable and must give account to God. God is love and God is just. So whether it is love, divine love you need, or justice you deserve, God is faithful and compassionate.

You will be well advised to "ponder in your heart" as Mary did the pattern of conduct God has set for you. If you honor it in obedience, you will learn more of God's love and you will not need to spend time before the seat of judgment for justice.

You may say, "I don't steal, beat up my wife, abuse my kids, lie, gamble..." etc. King Solomon's words are appropriate: "Catch the foxes for us, the little foxes that are ruining the vineyards, while our vineyards are in blossom" (Song 2:15 NAS). Little things, just a fraction, can spoil the whole. Adam ate fruit from the tree, thus there was spoilation and degradation, exposing the nakedness of Adam and his wife.

So our Heavenly Father cannot in any way or at any time suffer broadmindedness among His children, nor will He suffer a relaxing of His discretionary sovereignty. Man's prerogatives are expressed autocratically; he is a creature of his own making. His demeanor, his motives and his perspectives countervail the governance and sovereignty of the third Person of the Trinity.

The Holy Spirit is the first Person of the Godhead whom the sinner meets. It is He who brings conviction wherever sin is evidenced. If you have never been born again, you are lost, without hope, *dead*! You are a sinner in need of salvation and justification. This must take place before you are welcome in the presence of God the Father. You need a relationship with the Lord Jesus. God gave His only begotten Son out of love for mankind so that everyone believing in Him could receive everlasting life and not come into condemnation but pass from death unto life (see John 3:16). The knowledge of that truth inspires praise and rejoicing. "Let everything that has breath praise the LORD" (Ps. 150:6 NAS).

Let no one be lulled into a false sense of security by satan's oft-expressed lie that there are any number of ways to Heaven. God did not send His Son into the world for want of something to do. Rather, He is not willing that any should perish, but there is no hope apart from believing in Christ for salvation. God and His Son, the Lord Jesus, has finished His work. The rest is up to you. The ball is in your court.

5

One More Adam

Jesus Christ is the last Adam. He is Immanuel, "God with us." The first Adam failed his first test. God needed an Adam that would not fail.

Mary, the virgin daughter of Heli, of the tribe of Judah and of the lineage of David, is the instrument God used to introduce His Son to the world. The angel Gabriel announced to Mary the high honor which was hers, the promised benediction of praise among women and more importantly, her special and sanctified "favor with God" (Luke 1:28, 30).

The angelic visitation undoubtedly startled Mary and obviously she had questions, perhaps even some of a physical, biological, religious and political nature.

I believe it worthy of note that the first Adam, *when he was created* was virginal; pure and without sin. Great honor was imputed to Adam, who did not feel the understandable emotion of Mary. But Mary's ultimate response was, "Behold the handmaid of the Lord; be it unto me according to thy word" (Luke 1:38 KJV). Adam had no such response and unlike Mary, he disobeyed and invited God's disfavor. So we see that whatever God does is done with unsullied perfection. Everyone who is truly born again, born from above, is a virgin in the spiritual sense. God chose to use Adam and He chose to use the virgin Mary. He needed a clean, pure vessel, else His creative plan would be faulted.

Mary, believing as she did, had a minimum of questions. Her answer to the angel's message was given firmly and with assurance. But there was likely to be some bewilderment on Mary's part. She was a virgin from birth; she never knew a man. How would her husband react to this? Please note her response: "Behold, the bondslave of the Lord; *be it done to me according to your word*" (Luke 1:38 NAS).

Where Mary was bewildered, Eve was beguiled by that old serpent, who is called the devil and satan. Where Adam belabored the cause of his guilt, Mary believed the angel of Jehovah, who said, "For nothing will be impossible with God" (Luke 1:37 NAS).

There is the heart of the matter for Adam. God's instruction was simple and understandable. The Lord never complicates His message to His children with statements laced with ambiguities. So the question arises of why Adam erred. Was he hard of hearing or was he forgetful of what was expected of him?

Adam was capable of believing a lie, satan's lie. Thus he lost the sacred and exalted supremacy to which he held rightful ownership. A little lie is all that was necessary to steal from Adam the blessings God had promised him (see John 10:10). So we today are more than ready to believe the devil's lie, especially when we are challenged to live a life of consecration and sanctification, separated from the world that is under the control of satan.

The Redemptive Plan Unfolded

The first Adam lost his sanctification. How could it be recovered? With Adam and his wife, an animal had to be sacrificed in order to cover the nakedness of these people. Then they could be accepted into the presence of a loving God who is "not willing that any should perish..." (II Pet. 3:9 KJV). The next step occurred in Abraham's family. This time not an animal, but Abraham's own son, was to be the sacrifice. It tested Abraham's willingness to believe his God to the extent that should the son of Abraham be sacrificed, God was able to bring him back to life. Abraham was faithful and obeyed. Then an animal, a ram, was caught in the thicket. Let me quickly say a word concerning this ram. Any hunter familiar with wild animals will confirm the suggestion that wildlife is unlikely to be ensnared by brushes and surface growth, their natural habitat. The skeptic will argue this incident as one among many inconsistencies of the Word of God. Rams, especially, are familiar with their environment. But God does things in most inexplicable ways to serve His purposes. The perfect submission of and unmitigated obedience of Abraham to the command of God clearly showed Abraham and Isaac that

God will provide for every need. It revealed the omniscience and omnipotence of Abraham's God and our God, Jehovah Jireh.

But that was not the end. God had one more step to take in redeeming man to Himself, showing His grace and His love to the human soul, a love unfathomable, but forever true. God so loved the world that He gave His only begotten Son to die for sinful man, but unlike the animals mentioned earlier, the Lord Jesus Christ came forth from the grave, victorious over death and hell and in resurrection power and glory ascended to the Father in Heaven, to report to His Heavenly Father, "It is finished!" just as He announced from the cross for the world to hear (John 19:30). "...I have finished the work which thou gavest me to do" (John 17:4 KJV). The last Adam succeeded.

Our God-given Instructions

Before Christ Jesus returned to the Father in resurrection glory, He gave specific instructions to His disciples—simple, nonambivalent directions similar to God's instructions to Adam. What were these instructions? "...Go ye into all the world, and preach..." (Mark 16:15 KJV). Will it be easy to obey this command? Apparently so in those hearts where God-consciousness prevails. Unfortunately the churches of today are self-conscious, and "selfism" breeds lethargy.

A lethargic community seeks professional psychiatry rather than life-inspiring, life-giving work prompted by a knowledge of God's will and of a goal for life. A goal should fulfill what God has ordered for your life. When Jesus gave the command to His disciples to go, He never told them to come back.

Unfortunately, the churches suffer a kindergarten syndrome with ecumenistic paralysis. Our congregations have silent, secular saints who know little and do less.

We are not told the method satan used to enter the Garden. He was not included as one of the tenants from the beginning. Since I cannot believe God allowed satan's intrusion, the guilt must then be assigned to Adam.

God made the Garden of Eden for Adam and his progeny. Adam's guilt by disobedience forced his expulsion. Sin results in death. Satan knew what God had told Adam. But being the liar he is, he succeeded in getting Adam to believe the lie rather than the truth. However, as soon as Adam and Eve had eaten, their "eyes were opened...." Their God-consciousness was missing. Self-consciousness invaded, adding a new dimension to their lives. Then their nakedness, their shame, overwhelmed them and they tried hiding, but that didn't work.

One must conclude, then, that Adam did not believe. He was told specifically "to dress and to keep it" (Gen. 2:15 KJV). "Keep" is another word pregnant with meaning. It means to "hedge, guard, protect, attend to." Father Adam had his instructions as does every head of every family since then. The information given to every earthly father of every family is clearly stated with no options.

"Train up a child in the way he should go" (Prov. 22:6a KJV). This is a command to the husband/father. The mother is to nurse the child from conception to birth, and afterward with the assistance of the husband. His obligation is to nurture the child "in the discipline and instruction of the Lord" (Eph. 6:4 NAS).

The children are admonished to obey their parents *in the Lord, for this is right. Honor your father and mother, (which is the first commandment with a promise), that it may be well with you, and that you may live long on the earth"* (Eph. 6:1-3 NAS). It follows that the husband/father shirking his duties exacerbates problems for the child. This is most noted in our day. Children can be provoked "to anger" (Eph. 6:4 NAS). But today there are too many husbands and not enough fathers.

Adam's confession had four parts (Gen. 3:10). Two parts of the confession were internalized, two parts were externalized. That is a pattern for the sinner's confession to this day. Anyone outside the protection and the provision of God's grace has only one way to gain God's favor. Confess your sin (not your spouse's sin, your children's sin or even your pastor's sin) and believe in your heart. God will respond to your need, and your salvation is guaranteed.

6

The Messages of John

The works of the beloved apostle John, he "whom Jesus loved" (John 13:23 KJV), chronicled more of what Jesus said than what He did. John was the archivist chosen to relate Jesus' life and its relation to the long-promised Messiah of Israel, and ultimately of the whole world. The Holy Bible, the sacred volume, encompasses in entirety the God-breathed word, that word spoken through the patriarchs, the prophets, the kings and then the New Testament writers. "For no prophecy was ever made by an act of human will, but men moved by the Holy Spirit spoke from God" (2 Pet. 1:21 NAS).

The official document we as believers have, the Bible, was chronicled by those who had experience, or capacity for experience, who were open to spiritual illumination, who could absorb and obey the directives of the Holy Spirit and who evidenced energized devotion.

The apostle John, unlike any of the other writers of Holy Writ, was entrusted with the "whole counsel [purpose] of God" (Acts 20:27 NKJ).

John introduces his ministry by documenting his familiarity with what took place "in the beginning." He picks up his account there and the "angel of God" of Revelation 1:1 communicated to John the entire panorama of world history from the beginning to the end of time as recorded in his Gospel account, his Epistles and his Revelation.

The messages to the churches of the born again rabbi and apostle Paul were not overshadowed by the beloved John's assignment. Paul's messages were largely for the gentile believers while John's messages were directed largely to the Jewish population.

This conclusion may bestir inordinate concern among some fellow Christians. Consider this premise: Since the Church was not yet founded in the time of the apostle John, his recounting of the gospel was to predominantly Jewish hearers. (His three Epistles, full of profound inspiration for all, is the exception.) Even his message in the Book of Revelation begins by saying that it was what "God gave Him to show to His bond-servants [*doulos*]..." (Rev. 1:1 NAS). There are some in the Messianic Jewish community of believers who also give credence to the Book of Revelation being heavily weighted toward Israel.

Does anyone doubt John's presence when Jesus sent forth the "twelve" and "commanded them, saying, Go not into the way of the Gentiles and into any city of the Samaritans enter ye not: but go rather to the *lost sheep* of the house of Israel" (Matt. 10:5-6 KJV)? The same thesis was replicated where He specified, "I am not sent but unto the *lost sheep* of the house of Israel" (Matt. 15:24 KJV).

But did not John record the well-known verse of John 3:16? Yes, God loved the world, and was willing to go to great lengths to prove His point, even the death of His Son, often prophesied in their Scriptures. Israel corporately rejected the call of God and "crucified the Lord of glory" (I Cor. 2:8 KJV; see John 19:15).

The "Beloved Apostle" was in reality a disciple during the days and ministry of Christ. He was also the first male recorded as believing that Christ Jesus rose from the dead (John 20:1-8), and the first to recognize Him on the shore of Galilee (John 21:4-7). He was also entrusted with the care of Jesus' aging mother (John 19:26-27).

John as a disciple heard the principle of expectation carefully enunciated. With a readiness of mind and an intensity of purpose he matured into a dedicated hearer. The Lord Jesus motivated and molded His disciples into a viable faculty relationship. Hearing is a word with far-reaching and eloquent complexities. The first word in the litany of Jewish worship is the *Shema* or, "Hear, O Israel: The LORD our God is one LORD" (Deut 6:4 KJV). Hear is the word of the heart.

The point is that John heard with his heart; thus to him was given the assignment to tell the story from beginning to end. I find no difficulty with the Book of Revelation and its message being peculiarly assigned to Israel due to the usage of "bond-servants" (*doulos*, Gr.) The Greek word means "slave," one in "subjection" and one in "subserviency." This word is used characteristically of Israel throughout the Old Testament and a total of 14 times in Revelation.

It is a word befitting Israel. In his Gospel account and in the Revelation, John applies *doulos* 24 times, plus one (John 8:33). John, the ultimate Jew, addressed Israel with the future in mind. Israel will be under bondage until the Messiah appears. That is the theme of the Revelation, where he uses the word most often.

Speak the Truth

In every reference but one the word *doulos* is related to "bondage" and "servanthood." In the other place, John 8:33, the word *doulon* is the negative form. Here the Pharisees rejected the idea of bondage in any form whatsoever. Such rejection is in evidence so much today; rejection of what is set forth in the Scriptures. Very few messages from the pulpit challenge those in the pew with straightforward, finger-pointing, attention-getting reinforcements of the simple truths of the Bible. Too many men-pleasers and too few gospel preachers lead to a state of sinful relaxation. No reproach from the pulpit means no renewal in the pew.

The classic preacher or teacher who is an accredited student of the Word will apply his exegesis in a way that presents a critical explanation of the text or portion of Scripture he is teaching. (Exegesis means to extract the underlining meaning from the text.) That will be the guideline for your own private devotions and spiritual development.

On the other hand, if the preacher or teacher gives a faulty interpretation of a Bible text by reading his own ideas into it, whose views are more doctrinaire than fundamentally biblical, this person is known as an eisegete and is to be avoided. Cultists are among the greatest offenders. Unfortunately, they are not alone. Liberal humanists who find their way into many pulpits of America instill their soul-damning distortions of the Word of God into many.

We Christians need to know that we are not, as was Israel in their wanderings and in the Promised Land, "bond-servants." Instead we are "...joined to another, to Him who was raised from the dead, that we might bear fruit for God" (Rom. 7:4 NAS). There is now, since that joining, or marriage, no place open for us to allow other gods. The call echoes across the ramparts of time: Be holy. Acknowledge your sanctification. Be totally yielded to Him. Peter describes this process: "Since you have in obedience to the truth purified your souls for a sincere love of the brethren, fervently love one another from the heart, for you have been born again not of seed which is perishable but imperishable...through the living and abiding word of God" (1 Pet. 1:22-23 NAS).

In essence, "study to shew thyself approved unto God, a workman that needeth not to be ashamed, rightly dividing the word of truth" (II Tim. 2:15 KJV). Every classic biblical clinician will do so in order to substantiate his credentials as a scholar, professor, teacher or pastor.

So much of what one hears in Sunday morning services is void of sense and intelligence. We have the tear-jerkers, the comedians and even pulpit-thumpers and screamers. But after all the emotions are expressed and the ritual commotion is ended, the question surfaces: "What doth it profit, my brethren, though a man say he hath faith, and have not works?..." (James 2:14 KJV).

The ministers who are outspoken, straightforward and reliable in their exegesis of the Word will speak to pews that are full each service. Moreover, in my travels throughout the United States I have found a creditable number of this type of church that holds two and three morning services every Sunday.

Usually in either a local community of churches or a regional radio program, speakers will invariably have "sermonettes" that center around the parables or miracles found in one of the four Gospel accounts. These sermons tend to be a weak reading with a few asides and meaningless "words of wisdom."

Much of what one hears today in the name of fundamental preaching is shallow because the text is half-learned. The depth of the meaning is left untouched. By using some ambiguous "preacher phrases," the message is ended without mentioning the Heaven a believer can gain.

Worldly-wise "Christians," although participants in "the Lord's Prayer," reciting "Thy Kingdom come," are unaware that His Kingdom *has* come to the "spiritual virgin"—the believer whose life is at the beck and call of the Holy Spirit. That believer whose prayer is, "Lord, by Your Holy Spirit make me more God-like," is the one who will be like Mary and say, "...according to Your word."

7

In the World

Contrary to the song, this is not my Father's world...yet! But as surely as the sun rises each morning and sets each evening, a day is coming when satan will be cast out after his judgment is announced. But before someone writes me about it, let me answer the question, "What about Psalm 24:1?"

Are you familiar with the contextual setting of that verse? "The earth is the LORD's and the fulness thereof...." David here "sees" as John "saw" the end of days in Revelation. David "sees" the true David coming to the entrance of Zion in verse 3. This is millennium truth. "Who shall ascend...who shall stand...? He that hath clean hands and a pure heart..." (Ps. 24:3-4 KJV). God demands purity as evidenced in spiritual luminescence.

God knows you. He knows where you live. He knows what ensnares and enslaves you. He was never at a loss to know what His chosen people Israel were about or where they were. Time and again they are described with humiliating and agonizing words. They were "whores;" they were guilty of "whoredoms;" etc. All those and other terms show they were opponents of the God of Abraham, Isaac and Jacob.

You would be well advised when you learn that God expects, even demands, far more than He is currently receiving from those for whom Christ died and whom He desires to have in His family. The pattern has not been altered. When Adam disobeyed, all fell prey to satan's dominion. Satan gathered to himself and to his kingdom that which should never have been his.

Satan's Territory

Unlearned and unspiritual Christians do not comprehend the feverish activity of satan in our day. He knows that he has but a short time (Rev. 12:12).

Your Holy Spirit-sanctioned behavior undeniably places you in the direct line of satan's vicious and relentless attacks.

No, beloved reader and student, this world in which we all live is satan's domain. So we need to learn the fine art of coping with the archenemy of our souls. Praise be to our Heavenly Father and to the Lord Jesus, help is always near and ever present. "Yea, though I walk through the valley of the shadow of death, I will fear *no* evil: for thou art with me; thy rod and thy staff they comfort me" (Ps. 23:4 KJV).

For you see, God saw our need "from the beginning." Thus He accordingly provided the facility, amenity and advantage that we need for success in the on-going spiritual war with satan.

"For the Mighty One has done great things for me; and holy is His name" (Luke 1:49 NAS). That Name will never change. In it is permanency, continuity and divine superiority. But with that knowledge we still give control of our lives to others. We willingly become pawns, or puppets, in the affairs of life. That is sin at its most subtle level. But it will not likely remain on that level. Man's character must be prayerfully and carefully disciplined. Whenever sin, in any form, is allowed, there straightway follows an increase of velocity down the path to destruction.

The Pattern for Battle-ready Leaders

Listen to the Word of the Lord, O Church: "And I will betroth you to Me forever; yes, I will betroth you to Me in righteousness and in justice, in lovingkindness and in compassion, and I will betroth you to Me in faithfulness. Then you will know the LORD (Hos. 2:19-20 NAS). That is the leadership God promised to the children of Israel. You would be well advised to learn that God is no respecter of persons, especially when those persons are members of His family—those whom He has chosen for His own inheritance—Israel in former times and the believers who are members of His Body in this present dispensation of His grace.

Accordingly, the Holy Spirit made known to the apostle Paul His pattern for appointing persons to be on the front line, to be the battle-ready forces leading the attacks against "the serpent of old, who is the devil and satan" (Rev. 20:2 NAS).

The qualifications for these positions was every bit as restrictive in Paul's day as in Moses'. Paul, a knowledgeable scholar, knew the three-fold standard of the Torah in Exodus 18:21. That Paul was concerned with appointments made to the ministry is quite evident. "Lay hands suddenly on no man, neither be partaker of other men's sins: keep thyself pure" (I Tim. 5:22 KJV). The word "suddenly" suggests haste and insufficient testing. The word "pure" (*hagnos*, Gr.) is a piercing word; "Do not aid in sending unfit men into the ministry." The Church suffers because of this today as it did in Paul's day. Let all appointees to the ministry be proved [tested] and be blameless (1 Tim. 3:10).

All the patriarchal and levitical appointments had to be consecrated "according to the pattern." There could be no deviation from the divine directive. With these parameters inscribed in concrete, figuratively speaking, there could be no "quick fix" in the various assignments, where the human element could assert itself.

Whenever God's specific requirements are frustrated in the Church, in the business world or in the family, time will reveal a languishing and deteriorating in societal affairs. It is called by many names: recession, depression, hard times, etc. "For affliction [or any of the above] does not come from the dust, neither does trouble sprout from the ground, for man is born unto trouble as sparks fly upward" (Job 5:6-7 NAS). Do you fear the Lord? Do you obey the voice of His servant? Do you walk in the darkness with no light? "Let him trust in the name of the LORD and rely on his God" (Is. 50:10 NAS).

Are we the masters of our fate? If so, we have messed things up deliriously. Who's to blame? Visit your mirror.

When our Church leaders blatantly abandon the injunction to "preach the word" and speak the tangential, the Church has a problem, and so likewise will society. I am quite aware that this kind of talk is not popular. But I do have a calling and an obligation to my God, and He "sticketh closer than a brother" (Prov. 18:24 KJV).

Whether or not we want to believe it, the fact remains that something has gone awry in our present day leadership in the Church.

The Church at large has stood silently by, remaining quiet on such matters as abortion, aberrant sexual behavior, divorce of families and deceptive cults that prey upon our young people. Many of these groups purport to be the framers of a world devoid of problems that is presently a matter of great concern to myriads of people. The Church stands by, quarantined, speechless.

Do you believe God meant what He said about designated people filling places of responsibility in leadership? Paul, Moses and the patriarchs did. A pattern was presented to them which had to be faithfully observed.

Paul gave the Church this admonition: "Do not lay hands upon any one too hastily and thus share responsibility for the sins of others; keep yourself free from sin" (1 Tim. 5:22 NAS). "And let these also first be tested; then let them serve as deacons, *if* they are beyond reproach" (1 Tim. 3:10 NAS). "Do not neglect the spiritual gift within you, which was bestowed upon you through prophetic utterance with the laying on of hands by the presbytery" (1 Tim. 4:14 NAS). What more can I say?

At this point anyone may pray more intelligently and seriously, "Thy Kingdom come...."

This world, this age in which we are living, is resolutely, even obstinately, worsening day by day. Obstinately? Yes; for satan knows he has but a short time. "...Your adversary the devil, as a roaring lion, walketh about, seeking whom he may devour" (I Pet. 5:8 KJV). Be assured that he would devour you if he had the authority to do so. He certainly does not have the power to kill you.

Satan sought after Israel all through their journeyings. Many times he thought he had them and was ready to annihilate them. But God's grace prevailed. You may hear from the pulpits that you need not worry or be concerned with the devil. Do you have any scriptural credibility for that lie? James clearly enunciates in a profound statement: Submit to God...resist the devil! (James 4:7). Note the word "submit." That means give obeisance, which is a respectful gesture. That is submission. It is obeisance, not obstinance. You cannot adhere to things that displease God and still expect Him to hear you when you cry out for help. Satan will ensnare you if you tolerate him.

8

Choices for the Church

The pattern for the Church today is the same as it was for Moses in his day. At the advice of his father-in-law, Jethro, Moses circumscribed the choices for leadership of the children of Israel to a three-tiered standard: "...able men who fear God, men of truth, those who hate dishonest gain..." (Ex. 18:21 NAS). Moses was told to "provide" (KJV) those men for leadership. That word is translated variously in other versions, but quite literally the word means to "see," "contemplate with pleasure," "have a vision of," etc. In the appointment of laborers, all appointees must be seen to measure up to the biblical dictum, or authoritative requirements of Scripture. Every appointment must be made with the future in mind. Is the individual a person with vision? Does the appointee contemplate the assignment "with pleasure"?

This macrocosmic worldliness of leaders is seen in the repudiation of beliefs and doctrines once held inviolate. Fifteen or 18 minute sermonettes offer little or no antidote to satan's ills. The devil has not lost his ability to deceive. Just look at the statistics of an eroding church member roll.

Paul, in his letter to the Galatian church, made some pointed remarks expressing his concern if not judgment on their behavior as believers. (See Galatians 1:6-8; 3:1-5; 4:9-18; 5:1-4, 7.) Where were the leaders in this church and other churches established by Paul and for whom he held a spiritual paternalistic concern? We see that Paul had a true pastor's heart.

Christ's gift to the Church was without measure, "...that He might fill all things" (Eph. 4:10 NAS). "And He gave some as apostles, and some as prophets, and some as evangelists, and some as pastors and teachers, for the equipping of the saints for the work of service, to the building up of the body of Christ; until we all attain to the unity of the faith, and of the knowledge of the Son of God, to a mature man, to the measure of the stature which belongs to the fulness of Christ" (Eph. 4:11-13 NAS). Paul was not playing games, nor was he playing church, as so many are doing today.

Let me make note concerning the reference to pastors and teachers. The word used in the Greek for pastor is *poimen*. Strong's Concordance gives the explanation as "pastor or shepherd." The word for teacher is *didaskalos*, meaning "instructor or doctor." We derive the words *didache* and *didactic*, "fitted or intended to teach, one who conveys instruction" from *didaskalos*.

One of the reasons, if not the main reason, the Church is in a decline is the studied disregard for teaching. Teaching is a calling, and Paul made that the case for obvious reasons (Eph. 4:11-13).

Holiness Starts with the Believer

A careful and prayerful reading of the letters of the apostle Paul indicate something was wrong, in order to elicit his strong grievance with the affairs of the churches. He cried out not only to the church at Galatia, but also to the Corinthian church. To the church at Corinth he said, "I want to present you to Christ a pure virgin" (see Second Corinthians 11:2). God cannot use any but those who are virgins, spiritual virgins. Common sense dictates that most adults cannot qualify for biological or physiological virginity as the virgin Mary could and did so qualify.

Paul states with full assurance, "...for I betrothed you to one husband..." (2 Cor. 11:2 NAS). What we hear from most pulpits negates the absolute demands of Holy Writ. But there are no options. First Peter 1:16 quotes from Leviticus by saying, "Be ye holy; for I am holy" (KJV). "For I am the LORD your God. Consecrate yourselves therefore, and be holy; for I am holy. And you shall not make yourselves *unclean* with any swarming [creeping (KJV)] things that swarm on the earth" (Lev. 11:44; see also 19:2 and 20:7 NAS). What are the "swarming things" on the earth we are to avoid? They are those things that attract you, that appeal to your senses, illicit lifestyles, conduct unbecoming to a child of God. Satan is the mastermind at making desirable those things that lead to our ultimate destruction.

Today schools and educational systems across the country invest enormous sums of money in educating their students about the dangers of drugs. But the almost flippant manner in which illicit sexual behavior is discussed and the lack of behavioral refinement and low regard in which the teachers and scholastics are viewed is alarming.

A profusion of blame is available to be passed around, and usually it is to the wrong persons or government agencies where the finger of judgment is pointed. I beg to differ.

The *microcosm* of society is the Church. Yes, it does seem small. God, however, does great wonders with small things. "Do not be afraid, little flock, for your Father has chosen gladly to give you the kingdom" (Luke 12:32 NAS). God operates best with small things. For example, He used a staff in Moses' hand to convince Moses of His lordship (Ex. 4:2-3). Shamgar came with an ox goad and struck down 600 Philistines (Judg. 3:31). Gideon only had 300 men and some pitchers with torches in them, but he overwhelmed the armies of the Midianites and the Amalekites (Judg. 7). Mary had as her expression of faith: "For nothing will be impossible with God" (Luke 1:37 NAS).

Anyone who is sensitive to the message of the Scriptures and who is concerned for his or her own spiritual growth and growth in the Body of Christ need to hear the meat of the Word. The deeper meaning of the Word with its varied perspectives, when brought to the surface, adds immeasurably to one's spiritual underpinnings and understanding. Thus, "let your speech always be with grace, seasoned... with salt, so that you may know how you should respond to each person" (Col. 4:6 NAS).

Here is a vital component for the Body of Christ to practice. What is good conduct among believers will more than likely apply to your behavior within your own family, which should be the out-cropping of the seed planted by the pastor or Sunday school teacher.

Let's substitute one word in Ephesians 6:4: "And *pastors*, do not provoke your children to anger; but bring them up in the discipline and instruction of the Lord" (NAS). In the natural family environment, psychiatrists tell us that when early training in the home is neglected, when children do as they please, then later in their teen years they become "children of wrath" (KJV) or "anger" (NAS). Look about your home area today. Do you see what I see?

Several verbs to note are "provoke," "discipline" and "instruct." The words in translation suggest anger and rebuke as being necessary and, at times, urgent.

Although the apostle Paul addresses the matter of children, the application can easily be transferred to God's children. Here there is also a mild rebuke in correction.

The Church is presently at ease, but there are many problems seen in the Church. In former days, in my youth, the residents of any given city or town displayed a great concern for their house of worship. They contributed of their time, their talent and their tithes and offerings. Christian businessmen served on various boards and judiciously balanced the income with expenses while the pastor ministered to the spiritual needs of the congregation.

Tithing

The writer in a recent article in my local newspaper commented on a few statistics, one of which dealt with giving. According to these statistics, the amount of $300 to $400 was the average offering per member per year. Shame! Shame!

Most members do not conform to biblical standards in their giving. Ten percent is God's command. Too much? Consider what you pay on your credit cards...18 to 20 percent is the norm. Do not get caught up in that insane idea that the tithe was only for the children of Israel. You must make the decision of whether or not you will "rob God...[and be] cursed with a curse..." (Mal. 3:8-9 NAS). Or you can reap benefits promised by God, for if you are obedient, He will "open for you the windows of heaven, and pour out for you a blessing until there is no more need" (Mal. 3:10 NAS).

The message from the pulpits of our land is habitually silent on the subject of giving. The shocking truth is that empty pews cannot bring tithes to the storehouse. People are not hearing the right message.

No longer is the Church important to family life. We decide not to honor God with our tithes; therefore, the devourer can destroy the fruits of the ground...etc. (See Malachi 3:11.) Thus we have recession, resistance to and rejection of authority and ultimately rebellion.

The question may be raised: Who is this devourer that God speaks of in Malachi? Many things can ravage one's resources. There is illness, loss of employment, divorce, insatiable lust for "things," to name just a few.

Our Heavenly Father forever provides for His people with divine generosity. He is not a penny-pinching, miserly provider. That is man's picture of God, but he did not learn this from the Father.

Is this subject matter being discussed or even stressed as important in churches? Do you realize that more space is given in the Scriptures to money than to repentance? Tithing, with its concomitant enrichments is seldom spoken about, for fear, I suppose, of offending someone. Unfortunately, everyone loses with this ignorant and negative attitude toward money management.

9

Macrocosm Ravished— Microcosm Revived

The *macrocosm*, or the world at large in which we live, is desperately in need of help from the *microcosm*, the Church and ultimately the believers. Our leaders in government at the national level and the leaders of the nations of the world are faced with dilemmas for which no easy answers are found. They cannot provide solutions that would characterize Solomonic credibility. The Church has the textbook, and as such has believable answers.

Here is where, in my evaluation, the Church has "played the harlot" (Ezek. 16:28; 23:5; Hos. 2:5 NAS). God expected His chosen people Israel to be separate from, not a part of, the heathen nations around them. Paul chastened the Church of the New Testament for leniency when it should have asserted leadership and guidance.

The world leaders, more especially America's leaders, should have a compelling reason to seek out the "prophets" within the Church. It is inexcusable for the "salt [to] have lost his savour" (Matt. 5:13 KJV).

For example, on a recent national TV morning news program an author was interviewed on the substance of his book, titled *Nurturing Fathers*. This author sees, along with a great number of others, the necessity of and the value to the family when the father becomes personally involved with his wife in the rearing of their children. That is news? One needs only to read Exodus 20:5b to realize that God had the same idea thousands of years before. It may surprise people to find out that our God is "pretty smart." (You may note in this verse that mothers are not mentioned in context, and for good reason.)

Another segment of that particular TV program was devoted to the question of money-handling among students in the school. They discussed things like how to save a portion out of every paycheck and how best to invest so that the money works for you, the individual, and not that you work only for the money. More than two thousand school districts are initiating this program. However, our Heavenly Father enunciated the money problem a long time ago. We have a long way to go to rise to the level of God's clearly defined pattern. The corporate Church is under severe financial constraints because its members are not being taught God's program for money management. If we understood

God's arithmetic, many of our problems would evaporate. Believe it or not, the government leaders would then be ready to hear the reasons for our success.

Mankind's constant disobedience is the cause of all his problems in the microcosm of the Church, in the macrocosm of the world and on average in the family. People's humanistic selfism is not about to reflect favorably upon something not acceptable among their peers, for in the world "every man's way is right in his own eyes" (Prov. 21:2a NAS). Paul, in writing to the churches in Corinth, Philippi and Thessalonica, did not hesitate to admonish the people to "follow" him (I Cor. 4:16; 11:1; Phil. 3:17; I Thess. 1:6 KJV). Paul's was the voice of reason that clearly understood the pattern of conduct. In fact, he tells the Philippian church, "Brethren, be followers together of me...as ye have us for an ensample" (Phil. 3:17 KJV). The word "ensample" translated from the Greek word *tupos* is idiomatic of "the die was cast" and "he had the stamp of God's approval...." This is the voice of a great man with spiritual insight. Paul had biblically ingrained assurance; he was quite well taught in the Torah, the Tanach or all the prophetic writings then available. He was indeed God's man in God's vineyard doing God's bidding for God's glory and to the praise of Jesus Christ, with the full and unwavering guidance of the Holy Spirit.

Such credentials did not allow for vacillation or indecision in Paul's ministry. One might say in the language of today that Paul was one of the leaner and meaner evangelists or preachers of the time. His credentials before and after the call of God upon his life were impeccable and unimpeachable.

One must look far and wide today for the "men of the cloth" who will aspire to the pattern so assiduously observed by Paul and the other apostles.

Word-based Sermons

The faithful church-goer, the regular attendee at the weekly (or should that word be spelled "weakly") services seldom leave the premises of their church excited, inspired and blessed like Mary was when she heard the Word of God from the mouths of the angel Gabriel and Elizabeth. The news Mary received was revealing, it was expansive and interpretable, for she saw a transcendent, divine beneficence which embraced past history and yet would continue forever. "As He spoke to our fathers, to Abraham and his offspring forever" (Luke 1:55 NAS).

The Word of God abounds with messages that challenge the hearer to both functional and spiritual development and maturation. We Christians must realize that we belong to the Lord, we were chosen by Him and "appointed...[to] go and bear fruit..." (John 15:16 NAS). I see this as a command without options.

How often are you challenged after hearing the sermon of the week? How many times have you heard what Israel heard so often: "And now, Israel, what does the LORD your God require from you, but to fear [reverence] the LORD your God, to walk in all His ways and love Him, and to serve the LORD your God with all your heart and with all your soul, and to keep the LORD'S commandments and His statutes which I am commanding you today *for your good*?" (Deut. 10:12-13 NAS).

King David, the prophet Malachi and the apostle Paul all portray a God who is faithful and loyal, not transient or fickle. It behooves all who are believers to have spiritual capital and resources upon which we can bank with assurance (Ps. 110:4a; Mal. 3:6a; Heb. 13:8 NAS).

Christian Zeal

A man whom I greatly respect, Jack Van Impe, recently stated that he sees "a growing attack of intolerance and hostility against Christians." The heroes of the home screen vomit out profanities, deviant behavior, murders, rapes, robberies, etc. each day. Are the Christians enraged, or even distressed, as they daily watch about eight hours of TV? Are men of the cloth offended to the point where they vigorously expose these sins? In times past the men of God stood tall and fearless against the evils of their day. They "ran a tight ship" and history attests to their successes.

Consider the military forces. The academies and training bases of the Air Force, the Navy, the Army and the Marine Corps provide a cadre of men and women, commissioned and noncommissioned officers, around whom new recruits may be formed. In every case they are a singularly disciplined group of people who perform to a high degree of excellence and take pride in their accomplishment.

The leaders in the Church would be well advised to emulate this aspect of the military. It would be a blessing of epic proportions to the world. This would slow the inordinate growth pattern of Islam, the New Age movement and other false religions which attract many from denominational communities. If you talk to any in necromancy, black magic, sorcery, witchcraft, satanism, fortune telling, etc., invariably you will find them saying that they had Christian parents, they attended Sunday school or they were members of some church.

After some extended discussion between myself and a knowledgeable person on this and related topics, we concluded, "My goodness, there rests upon our preachers and other leaders in the Church a sobering liability, since people's eternal interests are on the line."

God has provided the pattern, carefully laid out for every one of us. "So then each one of us shall give account of himself to God" (Rom. 14:12 NAS).

There is no possibility, ever, of one of the members of the army or navy of the Lord being sent to the "brig" or other place of confinement for the crime of shirking the duties given into his or her command (although the idea has merit). In reality, we need to "get our act together" while we have the opportunity to do so. I use the word "we" in the broadest sense. Every believer will stand before the *bema* and "appear before the judgment seat of Christ [*bema*], that each one may be recompensed for his deeds in the body, according to what he has done, whether good or bad" (2 Cor. 5:10 NAS).

10

Out of Touch with Bible Reality

In recent times a number of preachers, evangelists and others in the Church have been grouped together and catalogued as "fallen leaders." Unfortunately, we could see no overflowing concern expressed for those who ostensibly were our brothers in Christ.

The parable of the Good Samaritan has an applicable storyline: "…'A certain man…fell among robbers…'" (Luke 10:30 NAS). That is a stratagem among many in satan's larcenous activities. He has a repertory of nasty tricks, such as stealing, killing and destroying (John 10:10).

The priest, the Levite, or the "religionists," prejudiced that "certain man," bypassing him by non-involvement in his problem.

But a "certain Samaritan," himself on a journey, having a schedule to fulfill, no doubt with time limitations, saw a man in need. He interrupted his plans when he saw a man in need. Arrangements were made with the innkeeper for housing and whatever else was needed. He invested two denarii, or the equivalent of two days' wages, with an assurance that any additional costs would be his responsibility to pay. The storyline concludes with a question and a command. "Go and do the same [likewise]" (Luke 10:37 NAS). Cynically speaking, that Good Samaritan idea won't work today. Rather, we manifest a spirit of abandonment, since we are not our brothers' keepers. The "Good Samaritan" syndrome is passé for our day.

Sadly, our present day educative process avoids the important familial issues of caring, restoration and deliverance. The Church is in a state of disarray. The graduate has a sheepskin or stunning parchment hanging on the wall, the mark of excellence attained. Is this process working for the common good? Or is it just for recognition? Paul says, "Therefore I run in such a way, as not without aim; I box in such a way, as not beating the air" (1 Cor. 9:26 NAS). The suggestion of "windbag" comes to my mind; "Always learning and never able to come to the knowledge of the truth" (2 Tim. 3:7 NAS).

God has outlined for us the reality of leadership. "Furthermore, you shall select out of all the people able men who fear God, men of truth, those who hate dishonest gain; and you shall place these over them, as leaders of thousands, of hundreds, of fifties and of tens" (Ex. 18:21 NAS). "These are they who were called of [from] the congregation, the leaders of their fathers' tribes; they were the heads of divisions of Israel" (Num. 1:16 NAS).

Leadership is an exalted position. It is not an activist position where one encourages self-gratification and personal exaltation to the detriment of others. The friends of Korah and Korah himself with 250 leaders of the congregation tried to do just that. But in God's sight their conduct was reprehensible. God had to initiate "instant judgment" (Num. 16:21). "Depart now from the tents of these wicked men, and touch nothing that belongs to them, lest you be swept away in all their sin" (Num. 16:26 NAS). Man does not realize that one of the distinctive characteristics of God is that He is, by His own statement, a jealous God (Ex. 20:5). More especially, I think, He is concerned that those in leadership be "men who fear God, men of truth, those who hate dishonest gain [whether personal or monetary]..." (Ex. 18:21 NAS).

So some of the "fallen leaders" of today have suggested in retrospect that pride intruded their lives, that they gave credence unwittingly and that they lacked spiritual awareness of offensive strategies against a hostile and treacherous enemy, satan. Thus they fell prey to a psycho-organic misfunction satan engineered with the obvious intent "to steal, and to kill, and to destroy" (John 10:10 KJV). These men conclude, quite honestly, that they were unaware of this treasonist saboteur at work in their lives and ministry.

The Facts about Our Victory

We should know that the tactics of the enemy are not fair. With satan anything goes, so long as it is in agreement with his plan. He knows we believers are in the world, which is his bailiwick. Being intruders, he must "wipe us out." However, he has overlooked that "no weapon that is formed against [us] shall prosper..." (Is. 54:17 NAS). He certainly has ignored the last two chapters of the Book of Revelation, where we win and he loses. Satan is spiritually and mentally retarded, a loser; we as believers are overcomers. All the weaponry, all the armament and the actual manual of warfare, the Bible, is in our possession. So what are we waiting for? Or did some of us not know this?

The Church and its membership will continue to be victimized and enslaved by whatever or to whomever we pledge our allegiance. Of course, you need to know whether or not you are saved. The assurance of your salvation is secured by the Holy Spirit. Do you realize that many Christians face the problem of not knowing? You must know you are saved.

The point is, Christ Jesus' coming to this earth manifested unmitigated intrusion into satan's domain. The world was satan's because Adam sold out to him. But it was not satan's from the "beginning" (1 John 3:8). From the "beginning" satan was deserving of death, spiritual death. Believers will be encouraged to know that and they must understand it. Christ rendered satan powerless. Christ "...disarmed the rulers and authorities, He made a public display of them, having triumphed over them through Him" (Col. 2:15 NAS).

The people in the church pew need to know these facts if they are to live a victorious life. The abnormality in the Church today is the lack of sound Bible teaching, teaching that is strictly from the Bible and not from some book written by an unknown author. The Bible is the textbook.

Proper Training in the Church

Moses was educated in the best schools of Egypt. He was the son of the pharaoh's daughter...what else would you expect? When leading the children of Israel, Moses was the pedagogue for Aaron, Joshua and others. Moses instituted properly documented and trained leadership.

Unfortunately, people today become disgruntled because sound teaching in the Church is lacking or at best, handled haphazardly. So people break away and wander aimlessly, not knowing where to go. They are easy targets for the many cults and "isms". Admittedly, these cultic bands of missionary marauders are enthusiastic in their work, eloquent in speech and knowledgeable of what they believe.

Others know the basics of these cultic religions and reject their doctrinaire writings and their verbal semantics. It is not uncommon to find these unchurched people facing a dilemma. Do they or do they not start a church of their own? Thus we have another splinter group, small in number and with only the remotest possibilities for growth. With some books from which they amassed some knowledge they are ready to conquer the world.

Yes, I know the New Testament churches met in people's homes and with some success. But let me tell you a little secret. When I was touring the Asia Minor areas where Paul founded these churches, our tour guide, a Greek lady, well versed in the Scriptures, never once pointed out to me, nor to anyone else that I was aware of, any church at Corinth, Galatia, Ephesus, etc. No reference was made to the churches in that area and I heard no questions asked.

Anyone who heard the call from the Lord to preach should first seek out a school of learning with a Bible-oriented course, a Spirit-filled faculty and a sound curriculum that allows growth in the things of the Lord. Anyone would fare quite well in most of the many Bible institutes in North America (Moody in Chicago; Prairie Bible in Canada). Many of these schools have provided the Church with supportable and tolerable leadership. There are many instances of graduates of Bible schools, etc., then advancing their eduction by matriculating into schools of higher learning. They had a desire for greater academic fulfillment which could be acquired only at the larger, more encyclopedic schools or universities where a greater universality and range of subjects exists.

With a solid base of intense Bible study received at a Bible institute or Bible college, one has substantial currency to stand and command others to stand, as Paul at Lystra "said with a loud voice, 'Stand upright on your feet.' And he leaped up and began to walk" (Acts 14:10 NAS). This magnanimous soul, this man chosen by God was used so singularly in teaching the converts and in establishing the churches. It is from his letters that the Church of our day gleans so much that is so useful and useable. Why? Some credit must redound to his earlier days as academician and chief rabbi.

The call to Paul was, "But arise, and stand on your feet; for this purpose I have appeared to you, to appoint you a minister and a witness..." (Acts 26:16 NAS). These were not meaningless words; they were spoken by the Lord Jesus. So Paul in turn admonishes the Ephesian church, "You need to stand firm. You need the full armor of God. There are rulers, powers and spiritual wickedness." (See Ephesians 6:11-12.) Moreover, he wants the Colossian church to "stand perfect and fully assured in all the will of God" (Col. 4:12 NAS). To the Thessalonian church he says, "So then, brethren, stand firm and hold to the traditions which you were taught [like in the Bible institute], whether by word of mouth or by letter from us" (2 Thess. 2:15 NAS).

Here is the "buzz" word: stand. This capability exists only when you are encapsuled, as Mary was, with the Spirit of God. Then and only then is fulfilled what Christ said to the disciples, "...the kingdom of God is within you" (Luke 17:21 KJV). His disciples were looking, no doubt as were the Pharisees, for some spectacular sign. Their speculations time and again proved their humanistic weather vane to be more specious than specific. Although they heard the Master Teacher who spoke to them with characteristic candor, they had a mindset that was not to be faulted. Someone has said the seven words most often heard or uttered are, "We never heard it that way before."

Correct "Handling" in the Church

Warriors are needed but are in short supply. David, who was a great warrior, had to call upon help to assist him. Observe these fighters: "...men of might, and men of war fit for the battle, that could handle shield and buckler, whose faces were like the faces of lions, and were as swift as the roes upon the mountains" (I Chron. 12:8 KJV). When Amaziah went to battle against the Edomites, he called for and got 300 thousand "choice men, able to go forth to war, that could handle spear and shield" (II Chron. 25:5 KJV).

The above warriors were remembered for their tenacity of purpose and their skill in handling weaponry. The enemy was present, so they had to fight or faint.

The apostle John said very simply, but with profound intelligence, "...our hands have *handled*, of the Word of life" (I John 1:1 KJV).

The apostle Paul wrote to the Corinthian church: "Therefore seeing we have this ministry, as we have received mercy, we faint not; but have renounced the hidden things of dishonesty, not walking in craftiness, nor *handling* the word of God deceitfully; but by manifestation of the truth commending ourselves to every man's conscience in the sight of God" (II Cor. 4:1-2 KJV).

Leadership in the Family

The husband and father also has a leadership position. Yes, upon the husband/father rests the obligation of nurturing and training the children in discipline and in love. Strangely, but surely, the father is the head of the family, and to the fathers is given the strongest admonition and injunction mandated not by any religious leader, church body or governmental body, but by God Himself. It is strongly worded and does not allow any freedom of choice. It is, in effect, a legal order. God demands cooperation from the family head. Disobedience results in a subpoena directed to your attention. "...For judgment [must] begin with the household of God..." (1 Pet. 4:17 NAS).

Just as He authorizes your headship of the household, so He is always ready and willing to help you. He will never leave you nor will He forsake you, whatever the obstacle or adversity (Heb. 13:5). One of today's problems, of mammoth proportions, is too many husbands and a dearth of fathers. Our society is full of one-parent families with the father paying child support or, worse still, the government assuming responsibility for the wife and children.

Every man whose conduct involves a woman becoming pregnant has affected that woman for life. The man is absent, but will always be the guilty party. He too must bear the responsibility for those children. Too many young people are left to fend for themselves. They become active in the drug culture. They resort to sexual lifestyles. Such perverted societal behavior will invariably lead to thefts, murders, suicides and just plain rebellion. You, fathers, will either bring up your children in the nurture and discipline of the Lord or provoke your children to anger, according to God's Word. Those are your options. God laid down the gauntlet; be obedient to His Word or be prepared for combat. Your disobedience will result in death, bloodletting, rebellion, lawlessness, etc.

In recent days, perhaps more now than at other times, we as a people have put on a spectacularly comedic show of the old Adamic nature that is still alive and active. When Adam tried to put the blame for his fall on Eve, it was, to his chagrin, thwarted by God. In America today we blame everyone but ourselves (we who are believers) for the economic stagnation, for the loss of jobs, for the lack of leadership religiously, politically, ecologically, financially, industrially and more importantly, spiritually. We can try battering other nations for their sensitivity to their leaders, their dedication to the work ethic, their enthusiasm on the production lines and their ability to produce with manifest pride. But we have tried to lay the blame for our lack of success where it does not belong.

Concerning the family structure, Moses was told that God visits "the iniquities of the fathers upon the children unto the third and fourth generation..." (Ex. 20:5 KJV). "The rest of the story" is to be found in the pulpits of the land. The family structure, or should I say, families with structural fatigue, are afflicted by inertia and immobility. The family unit is but the microcosm of the Church.

Confront Sin

There was a time when sin was dealt with, no holds barred. A preacher of bygone days preached one powerful sermon after another under the unction of the Holy Spirit. Sermons had such titles as "Sinners in the Hands of an Angry God." Reports about that kind of sermon said those in the pews rushed forward to the altar in a repentant attitude, pleading for the mercy of God and seeking the way to salvation. The way of salvation, the biblical pattern, was preached with fervor and conviction. The preacher himself believed there to be only one way to the heart of God, and that was by faith in the Lord Jesus Christ and complete reliance upon the Holy Spirit who leads into all truth.

I have difficulties with present day preachers whose capital emphasis is "Do good, be good to each other, pay your dues to the church, attend church as often as possible." In other words, "Embrace these imperatives of secular humanism." That way friends and neighbors will accept you as a "good person," a complete Christian whose conduct is to be emulated. Where, oh where, is the cry heard from the pulpit that calls to remembrance the sins of the flesh?

Preacher and pew alike must have a sense that sin is present and, unfortunately, it is countenanced with but little or no disappointment or genuine concern.

I said pulpit *and* pew and that is most unfortunate. The messages from the "sacred desk" are by and large empty words. They barely mention the sins so rampant in society today to those occupying the pews. Actually, many of those pews are empty. The psalmist speaks of "leanness of soul" (106:15), but why? "They soon forgot His works; they did not wait for His counsel, but lusted exceedingly in the wilderness, and tested God in the desert. And He gave them their request" (Ps. 106:13-15a NKJ).

Is not the world a wilderness? Is not the world, apart from the Holy Spirit, a desert? Man consistently tests, or tempts, God. That reference must mean the Christians of our day, the complacent, contented church members. Or perhaps I might say it refers to the complacent preacher who is soft on sin, to the indulgent deacons, board members and Sunday school teachers, all who are generally too courteous and conformable to denominationally-inspired doctrinaire but who are spiritually shabby and noncommunicative in scriptural doctrine.

Learn for Yourself

"Look! You are trusting in the staff of this broken reed, Egypt, on which if a man leans, it will go into his hand and pierce it..." (Isa. 36:6 NKJ). "Trust in the LORD with all thine heart; and lean not unto thine own understanding" (Prov. 3:5 KJV). Lean on no one, not the accouterment of the office of bishop, overseer or pastor, unless they are faithful to the inerrant Word of God. We cannot depend on others for learning the Word ourselves.

For example, for the redemption of mankind God chose a virgin and entrusted her as the depository of His Kingdom here on earth. That is so profound a body of truth that one might safely say it is hidden from the eyes and understanding of most. Christians need to find such truths in the Word themselves.

John of a certainty "saw" and tells us so (1 John 1:1); the apostle Paul "saw" and affirms (Acts 9:18). Even the blind man "saw" (John 9:18). Paul's prayer for the Ephesians was that "the eyes of your heart may be enlightened, so that you may know what is the hope of His calling, what are the riches of the glory of *his* inheritance *in* the saints" (Eph. 1:18 NAS).

Do you see developing in the Church the like of which Isaiah observed in his day? At that time a false image was portrayed by the evil powers represented in Damascus and Samaria. It resulted in Israel rapidly becoming a party to the corrupting morals present around it. That phenomenon could not be tolerated in Israel. The prophet Isaiah's great call to Israel in that day is the message of the Holy Spirit in our day. In short, it is to try everything by the Word of God.

Anything contrary to or less than the message of the Word of God, the written revelation of God, is of satan and not of the Holy Spirit. This is "the true Light, which lighteth every man that cometh into the world" (John 1:9 KJV).

All, then, who refuse to live in the light of God's Word will walk in spiritual darkness. They will be hungry and oppressed. Demon spirits will offer them help, but satan and his emissaries are afflicted with the most advanced retardation, mental and spiritual. Neither satan nor his fallen angels have the capability to give sound or correct directives. The Lord Jesus depicts satan as a thief who has three things in mind: "to steal, and to kill, and to destroy" (John 10:10 KJV). The end result of his activity is the certainty of its incendiary mandate: the lake of fire and brimstone (Rev. 21:8).

Two Classes of Men

There is in evidence today a quality of evil of massive proportions. It is so well concealed and hidden from sight most of the time that the masses of people fail to realize or understand its incendiary nature. For example, take sexual promiscuity. Those who were duped into thinking that this quality of evil was just "physical coupling" will be rudely awakened one day to find their trysts were with an enemy. Society will discover that sin has wages and these wages are paid in due course and in full.

However, there is a heartening and invigorating side. There is an incandescence and radiant spiritual climate in which the believer in God and in His Son Jesus Christ moves about in society. So there are two classes of mankind. The one sets on fire for destructive purposes; the other lights a candle or turns on a light switch to dispel the darkness. The one is mischief in disguise, with certain disastrous results in its wings.

The other is a person with a sanctioned behavior—sanctioned and nurtured in fellowship with and in obedience to the leading of the Holy Spirit. Just being in that person's company is itself tantamount to therapeutic renewal.

So those who do not live in the light of God's Word will walk in darkness. They will wander aimlessly; they will be hungry and oppressed, similar to other heathen peoples. It is certain that they will fret themselves and be perplexed; they will trust in demon spirits and things like necromancy. Although such things promise help, they give none. " 'There is no peace for the wicked,' says the LORD" (Is. 48:22 NAS). They shall look for help everywhere, toward Heaven and on the earth and shall find none. But there is a bright side for Israel in Isaiah's message. Even though they walked in darkness, Israel will have one day seen a great light (Is. 9:2).

Isaiah's prophecies appeared harsh and very judgmental, but they were messages the people could understand and accept or ignore. They might acknowledge it as acceptable or they might abort it in totality. Neither our Heavenly Father nor the prophet Isaiah relieves you of the ability to choose. "And if it seem evil unto you to serve the LORD, choose you this day whom ye will serve; whether the gods which your fathers served that were on the other side of the flood, or the gods of the Amorites, in whose land ye dwell: but as for me and my house, we will serve the LORD" (Josh. 24:15 KJV).

11

A Return to God's Pattern

The organized church, according to recent statistics, has had a devastatingly severe erosion of membership from its rolls. I have not heard many voices questioning it. Few are looking for the cause of this lack of stewardship in the Church.

The Church must be led back to the Word of God. From this Word will shine forth the luminescence and glow of the Holy Spirit as He moves in and through the believers who obey.

Michael L. Brown, a true son of Abraham, a Messianic Hebrew who knows Yeshua HaMashiach personally, writes in his book *Whatever Happened to the Power of God*: "If the Spirit of God were to leave the earth today, 90% of all Christian ministry would continue unaffected" (Destiny Image, p. 166).

Believers are to shine. "And they that be wise shall shine..." (Dan. 12:3 KJV); "Let your light so shine before men..." (Matt. 5:16 KJV); "Then shall the righteous shine forth as the sun..." (Matt. 13:43 KJV). But you say, "I have no candle. I have no switch to turn on." Therein lies the problem in the Church. The clergymen in the pulpit today needs to preach the Word. Holy Spirit ministration will doubtlessly have salutary influence on the congregants. They are but the microcosm of that message surfacing from the pulpit.

The Pattern of Salvation

I am compelled to say that I do not believe that this body of truth, salvation, is adequately represented "according to the pattern" from the pulpits today. In Israel's case, God was forthright in His mandates on how they could maintain their relationship with Him. It involved their religious exercises, their interpersonal conduct and their relations with the heathen nations. Even their dietary laws were prescriptive, instructive and to be observed for their well-being. The pattern was a requisite to be honored with no modification.

With Israel one can easily find instances where they arranged their own standards in violation of God's pattern. I believe that with God, nothing avails but perfection.

Yes, the absolute power of the Holy Spirit is able to "make you perfect in every good work" (Heb. 13:21 KJV). The Greek word rendered "perfect" includes the meaning of "complete, thoroughly." Whether then in saving or equipping the believer to "every good work," the Holy Spirit must be allowed His divine right to do so.

Unless the Holy Spirit is permitted to do His work in bringing a person to a confession of sin and of the ultimate effect of sin, that person cannot claim salvation. The continuing appeal made by "pulpiteers," evangelists, personal workers, whoever, to "open your heart and invite Him in" misses the mark, in my opinion.

I believe the Lord Jesus Christ meant what He said here: "I glorified Thee on the earth, having accomplished the work which Thou has given Me to do. ... And I am no more in the world..." (John 17:4, 11 NAS). "But when He, the Spirit of truth, comes, He will guide you into all the truth; for He will not speak on His own initiative, but whatever He hears, He will speak; and He will disclose to you what is to come" (John 16:13 NAS).

The Church age is the time when the Holy Spirit is in ascendency. Nothing, but nothing, happens until one realizes this most important truth.

The Lord Jesus in His work, His finished work on the cross, effectuates completely and to the Father's satisfaction the "pattern" of eternal salvation as outlined as far back as the Garden of Eden. Blood had to be spilled for disobedient Adam's sin before God could have fellowship with him.

Accordingly, the "pattern" embraces the imperative of John 3:16. The re-birth of the sinner is mandatory. The fundamental reason the Lord Jesus shed His blood is, "...without shedding of blood there is no forgiveness" (Heb. 9:22 NAS). Thus the sinner's redemption in God's sight is finished.

Let's use the birth in the human family as an analogy. No birth can occur apart from the fealty of the father...the male component. In the same way the Father's fidelity was in evidence with Adam. His care and His concern for Adam's well-being was never in question. Adam in trouble prompted the Father's involvement in that problem, and a way was made to release Adam from his flawed condition. He was in that condition because he had disobeyed his instructions.

Responsibilities of the Family Head

The head of every family since then has his instructions as well. "Train up a child..." (Prov. 22:6 NAS). This word is specifically for the husband/father. God said, "I have the work cut out for the mother." The mother nurses the child from the moment of conception to its delivery, when the baby enters the world. From that moment onward, the child is dependent upon both the mother *and* the father.

When a helpless child is ushered into a very hostile environment, it is time for the husband/father to become painstakingly active, Christ-like and God-fearing. The father is confronted daily with awesome responsibilities which attend the admonition of the Lord, such as proper and godly discipline and instruction of the Lord. Whereas the period before the birth of the child was shared by mother and child, the responsibility now takes on a new dimension. Nursing the child is largely the mother's role; nurturing the child becomes an obligation of the husband/father (Eph. 6:1-4).

In Paul's letter to the church at Ephesus lies at least one key to the anger of the youth of today. (See Ephesians 6:4.) We may try to lay the blame on everyone else: the educational system, inner city neighborhoods, lack of employment, etc. However, the source of the problem is not outside the immediate family.

Shirking your duties, dear husband/father, procreates another shirker. Because Adam had a faulty memory, he forgot what God told him was his sphere of activity and duty and so failed. Man has not progressed to any measurable degree to this day. I can see why God might have repreated the phrase "after its kind" so often in Genesis chapter 1. You and I will see in our offspring what we have produced.

When the husband/fathers seek prescriptive easement from their God-appointed and God-ordered tasks in the family, they do so with the assurance that certain disastrous and catastrophic consequences will ensue which will assuredly affect their immediate families. The spillover into society is devastating. The electronic media and the printed pages are stark reminders of a world in turmoil.

God's Pattern of Provision and Atonement

God has made every provision from the beginning of time for the well-being of His children. He placed very few restrints upon man. Whenever the Heavenly Father enunciated a denial, He did so for man's pleasure and comfort. God sought an inter-relationship with man in order to share with man His abundant "joy unspeakable and glory" (I Pet. 1:8 KJV).

When we take a misguided step, in unbelief and disobedience, a price is assessed that needs to be paid. At the least it requires a confession of the guilt, to which there is a promise of redemption and restoration. However, some extenuating factors may cause God, in His wisdom, to close some doors previously opened. There are lessons we may learn from a few such instances.

Moses was one of the men who shared sovereign stature in the courts of Pharaoh in Egypt while the children of Israel occupied the land of Goshen. He was second in command to Pharaoh.

At that time there was a recession, or depression. A famine was in the land. Everyone was on strict rations. But God's people had enough to eat and to spare.

Here is a lesson for people in our day who fear economic recession or even depression. "A faithful man shall abound with blessings" (Prov. 28:20a KJV). "But my God shall supply *all* your need according to his riches in glory by Christ Jesus" (Phil. 4:19 KJV).

Moses was a man of stellar leadership qualifications. He held intensely to the articles of his faith, notwithstanding his having a seat of honor in the highest court of Egypt. "...Moses...refused to be called the son of Pharaoh's daughter; choosing rather to suffer affliction with the people of God, than to enjoy the pleasures of sin for a season; esteeming the reproach of Christ greater riches than the treasures in Egypt..." (Heb. 11:24-26 KJV).

All that we are told concerning Moses in the Book of Hebrews and in the Pentateuch exposes the possibility of a defect, something that displeased God. Moses disobeyed at one point, and was thus barred from entering the Promised Land. "Because ye trespassed against me [broke faith with Me, NAS] *among* the children of Israel at the waters of Meribah-Kadesh, in the wilderness of Zin; because ye sanctified me not [did not treat Me as holy, NAS] *in the midst* of the children of Israel"(Deut. 32:51 KJV).

What had Moses done that God found it necessary to mete out such seemingly harsh judgment? The words used are "trespassed" and "sanctified." "Trespassed" in the Hebrew idiom means to "cover up" and to "act covertly or treacherously." The word "sancitifed" means "to make a pronouncement or observation that somethig is clean ceremonially or morally." There seems to be little hard evidence from our viewpont, but then we cannot see the whole picture like God does. God is firm, omniscient and eternally the same (Mal. 3:6; Heb. 13:8; James 1:17).

Moses, King David and the apostle Paul were three men of God whom He used, whom He blessed mightily and whom He called to be great leaders. Yet Moses, David and Paul had murder in their backgrounds.

Moses acted covertly and treacherously, and apparently fell short with regard to cleanness either on the ceremonial or moral level.

A price had to be paid for their sins. Even though Moses' and Aaron's deaths could be considered premature, and whatever the reason for God's displeasure, they were not permitted entrance into the Promised Land. David, although a king, was not permitted to build the Temple at Jerusalem. Instead his son Solomon began and finished the construction of the Temple. Paul, however, came under the redemption and exoneration of the New Covenant, for his sin was paid for on the cross.

So with the honor of leadership in whatever setting, whether political or Church or family, comes awesome responsibilities that require faithfulness.

12

This Your Day

"If you had known, even you, especially in this your day, the things that make for your peace! But now they are hidden from your eyes" (Luke 19:42 NKJ). This poignant lament uttered by the Lord Jesus on that day, when He descended the Mount of Olives and approached the Temple Mount, may not be read with indifference on the part of the reader. It was, in the minds and hearts of those in the throng that day, a time for great rejoicing, or at least they thought so.

Three groups were in the entourage that day: the disciples, the religionists and those singing the praises of Zion. The disciples were bewildered. Their Master was riding on the back of a lowly colt. He should have been riding a white horse like a king, since He was, they thought, coming into Jerusalem to take up a kingly residence, as prophesied by David (Ps. 118:26). But the Pharisees were rebuking Christ. The crowd was too disorderly for them. They were summarily told that if the multitude kept quiet, the stones would shout ecstatically and praise Him (Luke 19:40).

In all the excitement, and with the bewilderment and blindness of the disciples, Jesus *wept*.

Here the glory of the Lord comes to His vacant Temple after more than 400 years. For before Israel was taken captive to Babylon, the prophet Ezekiel recounted the incident of the glory of the Lord departing the Temple (Ezek. 10:18, 19; 11:22-25). Now the Lord returns, weeping! Nearing the climax of His ministry on earth, urgency and excitement dominate the scene. Luke also highlights a few incidents at this time which gripped the disciples with great wonder and astonishment.

First is the incident where the rich young ruler approached Christ, very deeply concerned about his eternal welfare and, no doubt, his then-present lifestyle (Luke 18:18ff.). Mark says in his account that this young man came "running" to Jesus (Mark 10:17 NJV). Then we have Zacchaeus who was "little of stature" (Luke 19:3 KJV). The word communicates urgency. The message was: "Zacchaeus, hurry...*today*..." (v. 5 NAS). What was Zacchaeus' response? He hurried, he came down, he received Him joyfully. Did the Lord require anything from him? No! But Zacchaeus freely offered "...half of my goods I give to the poor; and if I have taken any thing from any man by false accusation, I restore him fourfold" (v. 8 KJV). That was 400 percent! Talk about excitement and urgency! It is all there.

The euphoria among the followers continues, but this time the outcome is somewhat different. Christ ascends the Mount of Olives, followed by a crowd...a mix of children, true followers and the religionists.

"If you had known...." The words of the Lord Jesus here are, I believe, the most heart-rending, the most excruciating, that ever fell from the lips of the Son of the Most High, who was to be given "the throne of his father David: and he shall reign over the house of Jacob for ever; and of his kingdom there shall be no end" (Luke 1:32-33 KJV).

To Hear and to Know

In a colloquy about parables that Christ had with the disciples, He answered, "To you it has been granted to *know* the mysteries of the kingdom of heaven, but to them it has not been granted...because while seeing they do not see, and while hearing they do not hear, nor do they understand" (Matt. 13:11-13 NAS). "For this people's heart is waxed gross, and their ears are dull of hearing, and *their* eyes *they* have closed" (Matt. 13:15a KJV). In this is fulfilled the prophecy of Isaiah 6:9-10. "And He said, 'Go, and tell this people: "Keep on listening, but do not perceive; keep on looking, but do not understand." Render the hearts of this people insensitive, their ears dull, and their eyes dim, lest they see with their eyes, hear with their ears, understand with their hearts, and repent and be healed' " (NAS).

The same is recounted by Paul in Acts. The writer of Hebrews, (I believe the writer was Paul), uses the same words. The nuances one sees in the Books of Matthew and Acts says, in effect, that those who were "dull" were "burdensome" to the spread of the gospel. They were a "load." In Hebrews (5:11) a different Greek word is used, still translated "dull," but with the added comment that these people were "sluggish, stupid and lazy."

I believe the Lord is saying, without equivocation, that if we are dull of hearing, then we fit into a pattern of inactivity expressed as "sluggish, stupid and lazy."

Loved ones, that is plain, non-flattering, easily understood language. Only a theologian can make it mean something different.

Within the context of Matthew chapter 13, I believe, one can readily see that no one is made to be alert to the Word of God. No one is forced nor constrained to give any heed whatsoever, nor must one obey the commands given by God and His messengers so long as that one is out of the family relationship. The change takes place when one becomes a family member. The believer's conduct takes on a new meaning when the Holy Spirit takes up residence in the heart. There is available a ready mentor. Not until He sets up His throne, and not until He occupies that throne, is it necessary for you to commit anything to Him.

You have a choice during this period of grace. You can have it your way. But you will find what the prophet Haggai found in a characteristically stingy

Israel. "Ye have sown much, and bring in little; ye eat, but ye have not enough; ye drink, but ye are not filled with drink; ye clothe you, but there is none warm; and he that earneth wages earneth wages to put it into a bag with holes" (Hag. 1:6 KJV).

And so Jesus weeps, having in mind, I can believe, the words of the psalmist, "Sacrifice and offering thou didst not desire; mine ears hast thou opened: burnt offering and sin offering hast thou not required" (Ps. 40:6 KJV). Jesus had poignant and profoundly heartfelt concern for those around Him on that day, "saying, If thou hadst known, *even thou*, at least in this thy [your] day, the things which belong unto thy peace! but now they are hid from thine eyes" (Luke 19:42 KJV).

The Return of God's Glory

"This *your* day." Yes, the day was made for them at that time, and with all the praising of God and rejoicing, they missed the significance of the Lord's returning to His Temple. As mentioned before, the glory of the Lord was present in the Tent of Meeting in patriarchal times and in Solomon's Temple, then it later departed, as Ezekiel related (Ezek. 10:18-19; 11:22-25). Now Christ was riding down the winding pathway of the Mount of Olives. The glory of the Lord was again about to enter the Temple, only to find it had been spiritually prostituted and had become a place of merchandise.

Let's consider Israel's return from captivity. Under Zerubbabel and Nehemiah, with assistance from others, Israel rebuilt...but without the glory of the Lord. Now those words of the Lord Jesus take on a new significance. Did Israel grasp this statement made by Christ? "...If thou hadst known, even thou [you], at least in this thy [your] day..." (Luke 19:42 KJV). It is *even you*, you, Israel, above all people...and *this is your day*.

Paul's words in a later day speak of this issue concerning Israel. "But their minds were hardened; for until this very day at the reading of the old covenant the same veil remains unlifted, because it is removed in Christ" (2 Cor. 3:14 NAS). Israel was then and still continues to be blind. Accordingly, Israel was removed as Adam in a former time was removed, not following the pattern.

God in His infinite wisdom saw fit to graft branches from a wild olive tree into the original tree so they might partake of the root and fatness of *the olive tree* (Rom. 11:17). Let us take heed. Has this ingrafted, wild olive tree branch demonstrated its trustworthiness? Or are the words of Christ applicable to it also?

13

Two Men on a Mission

To the serious-minded student, professor, scholar or pastor, there is a striking similarity in the exhortations and writings of two men in the New Testament Scriptures.

John and Paul were men of sublime and *empyreal* character. I use the word *empyreal* to describe men whose lives were circumscribed, surrounded by a warmth experienced through closeness of fellowship with their Lord (*empyreal*, Gr.; *en* or "in," and *pyro* "fire").

These men were consistently on the hot seat because of their dedication and obedience to the Word of God.

John was charged with the message of "in the beginning" (John 1:1, 3). He confirms this message in the latter years of his administration. "What was from the beginning, what we have heard, what we have seen with our eyes, what we beheld and our hands have handled, concerning the Word of Life ... what we have seen and heard we proclaim to you also, that you also may have fellowship with us; and indeed our fellowship is with the Father, and with His Son Jesus Christ" (1 John 1:1, 3 NAS).

Please note that John does not refer to the Holy Spirit in his introductory comment. Instead, for some reason, he holds back mention of the Holy Spirit until chapter 3, where he specificates, not speculates. "And the one who keeps His commandments abides in Him, and He in him. And we know by this that He abides in us, by the Spirit which He has given us" (1 John 3:24 NAS).

John's reference to the word "command" in its various forms is found at least 21 times in his Epistles and in the Revelation. This fact confirms to me that the burden of his heart was for his brethren in the flesh, Israel. In his Gospel account the Lord Jesus seldom refers to the commandments.

On the other hand, the heart of the apostle Paul for his brethren, poignantly expressed in Romans' parenthetical chapters of 9, 10 and 11, seems almost extremist since he, a Jew, was assigned to begin a ministry among the Gentiles (Acts 13:46-47).

The apostle John's writing was gripping and compulsive for those of his culture. Accordingly he recounted the events of the beginning and the longsuffering of a benevolent God despite the near insolvency of Israel throughout its history. He tells them that their troubles were from the beginning and it was time for change. Hence he calls their attention to the commandments and to the spectacular events about to transpire which he recorded in the Revelation.

The apostle Paul's ministry was one of church planting and building, although he at times could be "lean and mean." So then Paul went to the Gentile community, and John to the Jewish community.

God's Promises

The apostle John, a Jew, passionately addresses, as Christ did, this people with their problems and calls for obedience. This word was familiar to Israel. "Now then, if you will indeed obey My voice and keep My covenant, then you shall be My own possession among all the peoples, for all the earth is Mine" (Ex. 19:5 NAS). The covenant with Israel was inviolate, but disobedience by their non-observance was displeasing to God. Herein was their pattern.

However, God has not forgotten His people Israel, nor His promises made to them. These were covenant promises, and God is a covenant-keeping God. Both the prophet Malachi and the apostle Paul tell in so many words that God changes not and is the same yesterday today and forever (Mal. 3:6; Heb. 13:8). Paul does not tell us that the covenant and the promises made to Israel have been transferred to the Church. On the contrary, he says, "But now He has obtained a more excellent ministry, by as much as He is also the mediator of a better covenant, which has been enacted on better promises" (Heb. 8:6 NAS).

God's people, whether they are Israel or the Church, are given promises. Peter calls them "precious and magnificent promises" (1 Pet. 1:4 NAS). The promises are viable in perpetuity for Israel too. Why? "...They are beloved for the sake of the fathers" (Rom. 11:28b NAS).

Isaiah saw the fulfillment of these promises being carried out: "Open the gates, that the righteous nation may enter, the one that remains faithful" (26:2 NAS). "Who has heard such a thing? Who has seen such things? Can a land be born in one day? Can a nation be brought forth all at once? As *soon* as Zion travailed, she also brought forth her sons" (Is. 66:8 NAS).

Ah, many surprises are in store for the Christian who is un-taught in the Word. The sinners in the world, who know not the Lord Jesus as Savior, will also be unprepared for the realities spoken in the Word.

The Old Testament writers and the New Testament writers lived with eternity in mind. John was no different. His messages were always written with eternity in mind. And in his later writings he gives his summation addressing the commandments and the requirement to be obedient.

The apostle Paul, one of the more prolific writers of the New Testament, delivers the message of a pastor to the churches. He speaks with profundity, but always with the spiritual impact that the Word brings to bear. Yes, he got his materials for preaching from the Old

Testament, a portion of the Bible hardly ever called into play today.

There are times when God will use others "not of this fold" (John 10:16 NAS) to keep His promises and to convey His care for a listless, unconcerned people. For example, consider the words of Pharaoh of Egypt who expressed his concern for Joseph and his people by telling them not to worry, "I will give you the best of the land of Egypt" (Gen. 45:18 NAS). Egypt was in a state of famine, but there was no famine for Israel!

God knows when His people are in need, and will prepare for any eventuality. He will give you "of the dew of heaven, and of the fatness of the earth, and an abundance of grain and new wine; many peoples serve you, and nations bow down to you..." (Gen. 27:28-29 NAS).

Spiritual Purity

Perhaps what I am about to say may be disquieting for you, but I believe it needs to be said. God is scrupulous and discriminating in His choice of manpower. "Who maketh his angels spirits; his ministers a flaming fire" (Ps. 104:4 KJV). Take that pattern or standard of conduct to today's preachers. Do they fit the required measurements? For this matter, let me reintroduce the subject of virginity as it relates to the spiritual person.

When you say with the apostle Paul that you are born again and a new creation (II Cor. 5:17 NKJ), that new creation is within your heart. That phrase cannot mean that you are a new creation bodily. You have the same body with all its various components. You live and breathe as before, but changes will surface as the new resident, the Holy Spirit, gives you a different outlook, or uplook, on your life. He who is within you is greater "than he who is in the world" (1 John 4:4 NAS). This, then, is that spiritual virginity. It assuredly is not something physiological, or biological in essence, but is rather that which is of God. It became available to all believers in the Lord Jesus Christ after the crucifixion, death and resurrection of Christ. That was not available to Israel beforehand, but the prophets and writers in the Tanach (the Hebrew Scriptures, or the Old Testament) had had glimpses of this "new thing" spoken of by Isaiah (43:19) and looked forward in faith to that day.

Most, if not all, in the Church community have passed the phenomenon of biological and physiological virginity, but that does not invalidate the phenomenon of spiritual virginity for the child of God.

There are some personalities in the Scriptures whom I can believe were spiritual virgins. Adam, Abraham, Joseph in Potiphar's house, many of the prophets, etc. could be called spiritual virgins. Adam was in the beginning made perfect and without blemish. Paul was also spiritually pure and clean. John was likewise, and he records the words of Christ to the religionists, the Pharisees: "You are from below, I am from above; you are of this world; I am not of this world" (John 8:23 NAS).

However, there is an opposite to spiritual virginity as well (i.e., sexual obscenity). The term "spiritual whores" is used in both the Old Testament and the New Testament approximately 100 times, in various adjective, verb and noun forms. John uses the term six times, Paul twice. The meaning of the word in the Hebrew or the Greek speaks of unfaithfulness in desire. That was rather common among the Hebrew people throughout the Old Testament.

Believers today can also be blemished and even disfigured by having congenial relationships with those in the world. You must know that we are captives to whomever or to whatever we yield allegiance. Does this answer the problems today in our personal lives, in the Church, in the political bodies, etc.?

Carrying Out God's Purposes

Disregarding the commandments and continuing in disobedience and rebellion against the prophets complicates the reasons for Israel's being set aside. Their being set aside, or as the apostle Paul describes it, some of the branches being broken off, allowed the "wild olive, [to be] grafted in among them and [become] partaker with them of the rich root of the olive tree" (Rom. 11:17 NAS). But despite their meandering, God continues to love and care for Israel. Paul postulates the astonishing premise in Romans chapter 11 that even though they are enemies on your account, God says they are beloved on *account of the patriarchs*. "Our godly forefathers demonstrated their status with God," Paul says. Paul was familiar with the history of

Israel and this knowledge prompted him to be fearlessly vocal.

But a mutinous and murderous envy arose among the Jews from Iconium and Antioch, by which they "won over the multitudes, they stoned Paul and dragged him out of the city, supposing him to be dead" (Acts 14:19 NAS). Why shouldn't these from Antioch and Iconium have misgivings about Paul? Ananias had, until God told him that Paul was a "chosen instrument of Mine to bear My name before the Gentiles and kings and the sons of Israel" (Acts 9:15 NAS).

He was indeed a chosen instrument. God had many great things that He would accomplish through him. No amount of hatred, personal animus or threats of death could dissuade Paul from carrying out the purposes of God. God does not choose rubbish to carry out His will. He chose Mary, a virgin, and presented her with a natural and physiologically insurmountable proposition that had both religious and social ramifications. But Mary's answer suggests indifference to pleasure or pain in the matter: "...be it done to me according to your word" (Luke 1:38 NAS).

Paul's response mirrors that of Mary's to the angel Gabriel. Having received his eyesight, Paul was directed to "be filled with the Holy Spirit" (Acts 9:17 NAS). After three things, the laying on of hands, receiving eyesight and being filled with the Holy Spirit, he proceeded to the synagogue and said, "He is the Son of God" (Acts 9:17-20 NAS).

Perceiving the Kingdom

John records the essence of the Lord's high priestly prayer in John 17:16: "They are not of the world, even as I am not of the world" (NAS). This man was entrusted with a body of truth. He knew about the Kingdom of God, and addressed it in his Gospel account, beginning with the encounter Christ had with Nicodemus, the Pharisee. Today there is much talk and pontificating about the Kingdom of God.

Luke speaks forthrightly when he says that the Kingdom is not a happenstance or event which draws much attention. "The kingdom of God is not coming with signs to be observed...the kingdom of God is in your midst" (Luke 17:20b-21 NAS). I belive that whenever a life, yours or mine, is subservient to the will of God, there is in reality the Kingdom of God. For example, Mary was the envelope in which the Kingdom of God was operative. And although she has left no tangible legacy, she has never been forgotten. The apostles John and Paul were vehicles for the Kingdom of God. The legacy they have left us is beyond comprehension, for their works follow on centuries after their demise.

The apostle Paul both intrigues and challenges me in my daily life. He exemplifies the statement of the Lord Jesus in His word to those Pharisees, "the kingdom of God is in your midst" (Luke 17:21 NAS). Paul himself was a Pharisee, and I believe the Kingdom of God was "within" Paul, for he mentions the Kingdom at least 23 times in his writings. He reveals a perception of Kingdom teaching and doctrine.

The Kingdom is analogous to the Holy Spirit's being the driving force in one's life and in every activity of that life. When the Word states so clearly that the Kingdom of God is "within" us, I must believe that. That was central to Paul's preaching at Ephesus. He declares, "...I went about preaching the kingdom..." (Acts 20:25 NAS). What does he mean by that? "[I served] the Lord with all humility and with tears and with trials which came upon me through the plots of the Jews...declaring to you anything that was profitable...solemnly testifying to both Jews and Greeks of repentance toward God and faith in our Lord Jesus Christ" (Acts 20:19-21 NAS). "For the kingdom of God does not consist in words, but in power" (1 Cor. 4:20 NAS).

From Paul's firsthand knowledge of this awesomely challenging but rewarding ministry, there were very few who found this work attractive. He calls attention to the church at Colossae of the *small number* who were "fellow-workers for the kingdom of God..." (Col. 4:11 NAS). It's the same today. And that is the point to be emphasized. "For you have been called for this purpose, since Christ also suffered for you, leaving you an example for you to follow in His steps" (1 Pet. 2:21 NAS).

Spiritual Virginity

Do I believe Paul was a spiritual virgin? Emphatically yes! Before his confrontation with the Lord on the Damascus road, Paul was active in that supercilious group of pharisaical religionists. He did agree to the killing of Christians, of which he spoke afterward, "So then, I *thought to myself* that I had to do many things hostile to the name of Jesus of Nazareth" (Acts 26:9 NAS). But Paul had the witness within that he was that *new creation* he spoke about in Second Corinthians 5:17. It was workable and practical for him. He confirms his belief when he stands before the various tribunals. "...I cheerfully make my defense" (Acts 24:10 NAS). "...I also do my best to maintain always a blameless conscience both before God and before men" (Acts 24:16 NAS). "Brethren, I have lived my life with a perfectly good conscience before God up to this day" (Acts 23:1b NAS).

Here was a man who was a new creation. He could tell the church at Corinth, "For our proud confidence is this, the testimony of our conscience, that in holiness and godly sincerity, not in *fleshly wisdom* but in the grace of God, we have conducted ourselves in the world, and especially toward you" (2 Cor. 1:12 NAS). And later he said, "I thank God, whom I serve with a clear conscience..." (2 Tim. 1:3 NAS).

Nothing about his past created a stressful condition, either physical, mental or spiritual. He really believed he was a new man. That new creation was not the result of his "praying through," doing penance or any other man-devised course of action. He simply *believed* God, made a 180 degree turn and thereby became a member of God's family, withstanding satan at every turn. He had purity of heart, life and ministry in his sights at all times.

It might be said that the Corinthian church stood in the forefront as a church with loose morals. To this church Paul directed two lengthy letters. He ends his second letter by saying, "For I am jealous for you with a godly jealousy; for I betrothed you to one husband, that to Christ I might present you as a pure virgin" (2 Cor. 11:2 NAS).

So it is possible to be a chaste, pure virgin in the spiritual context.

The apostle John shows us the pathway to spiritual perfection in his first Epistle: "If we confess our sins, He is faithful and righteous to forgive us our sins and to cleanse us from all unrighteousness" (1 John 1:9 NAS). Paul no doubt was aware of this truth, for I believe the apostle John and Paul were friends. In any case, the matter of spiritual maturity and purity weighed heavily on these two great apostles.

Some find the idea of spiritual virginity hard to comprehend. Mary too had difficulty when she was informed that God would use her to introduce "a new thing" into the world. Still, she was obedient, despite encountering complexities of which the full extent she most certainly could not understand. The apostle Paul, from the human standpoint, had very little to gain in obeying the voice on the Damascus road. But he did, and we all know "the rest of the story."

God is looking today for one whom He can trust to do a "new thing." The Church is in desperate need of another Paul, John, Mary, Isaiah, Moses or Abraham. The field is not crowded; the fields are white unto harvest.

The Message for Israel

Many quasi-prophets were in Israel. They bore a slight resemblance to divinely appointed men, but had improper credentials. Many were within the priesthood, the religious community, both inside and outside Israel. They were not short on laws, for Israel had more than 600 laws of their own. These God-fearing prophets, knowing the severity of God's judgment, failed at every turn.

Alas! The availability of wise counseling was in short supply. In the history of God's chosen, indeed greatly beloved people, His covenant people, they are found to be faithless and unbelieving. That sin culminated in their being expelled from their land. Isaiah refers us to the reasons for chastisement: "...for they would not walk in his ways, neither were they obedient unto his law. Therefore he hath poured upon him the fury of his anger...yet he knew not; and it burned him, yet he laid it not to heart" (Is. 42:24-25 KJV). God did speak of His redemption of Israel in Isaiah 43:1-13 for the future, but at the time Israel was in no mood to yield to the allurements proposed by the prophets.

God tells Israel, and all others who will believe, that His mercy is infinite and perpetual.

His oft-expressed desire for Israel in their day was that they be His surrogate, His emissary and His legal practitioner on earth. That was God's way of announcing the coming of One who would be the Legal Practitioner in Heaven for all believers engaged in a lawsuit against satan, the "accuser of the brethren."

God's love, compassion and concern for Israel is presently in abatement, but not in abandonment. It is just a temporary suspension. Yes, many in Israel will die without a knowledge of sins being forgiven, but thank God, word is coming to the Church that many in Israel and around the world are accepting Jesus as Jeshua HaMashiach, as their Messiah. And so they will be in Heaven with the others who have believed.

Since the crucifixion and resurrection of Christ, and with the institution of the Church as recorded in the Book of the Acts of the Apostles, God has sought for affirmative action from the Church in correcting the current discrimination against the Jews brought on by Israel's illicit relationship with the nations and their disregard for and violations of their laws.

Now the Church is the *amicus curiae*, the friend of the court. We as believers take part with the Holy Spirit in bringing about the salvation and redemption of Israel.

That theme was of predominant and supreme importance to John and Paul. God has had from the beginning a "pattern" for every aspect of His Kingdom, in order for excuses and fault-finding to have no credence. The "pattern" found so often in the preachments and writings of these two stewards was entrusted to them because of their formidable spiritual faithfulness to the directives of the Holy Spirit.

Paul could say without equivocation or mental reservation whatsoever: "Brethren, join in following my example, and observe those who walk according to the *pattern* you have in us" (Phil. 3:17 NAS). "...That in me *first* Jesus Christ might show forth all longsuffering, for a *pattern* to them which should hereafter believe on him to life everlasting" (I Tim. 1:16 KJV). "Not because we have not power, but to make ourselves an ensample [pattern] unto you to follow us" (II Thess. 3:9 KJV). "For I gave you an example [pattern] that you also should do as I did to you" (John 13:15 NAS). "In all things show yourself to be an example [pattern] of good deeds, with purity in doctrine, dignified, sound in speech which is beyond reproach, in order that the opponent may be put to shame, having nothing bad to say about us" (Titus 2:7-8 NAS).

14

Speak Up, Church.

The preacher who soft pedals on the sins of society is no worse and no better than the "influence" peddlers in the political and professional domain. The apostle Peter inquired of the Lord one day, *quo va'dis?* "Whither are you going?" It is a timely question to pose to many of the ministers of our churches. Where, indeed, are you going?

The U.S. government has almost succeeded in depriving the school system of the privilege of allowing Scripture reading and giving invitations to Bible studies in the schools. The list of prohibitions concerning the Bible increases day by day somewhere in our country, a supposedly "Christian" nation founded upon Judeo-Christian principles.

Has the Church lost its mooring? Is the Church no longer a mouthpiece to the world because of myopic astigmatism? Does the Church not hear a Macedonian call like Paul's (Acts 16:9)? Do our churches not hear, can they not see? "They" means all of us. Inertia abounds, with seemingly uncontrollable consequences. Those in the pew are not being told that sin must be repulsed by word and by action. Have you lately expressed your thoughts about what is happening in your school, in your community and in the Church?

The Church is moving too slowly in evangelizing the community of which it is a part. "Behold, the day of the LORD is coming, cruel, with fury and burning anger, to make the land a desolation; and He will exterminate its sinners from it" (Is. 13:9 NAS).

That verse devastates the unstable proverb, "God hates sin, but He loves the sinner." Why then would Isaiah say something different? Furthermore, why should God destroy both Sodom and Gomorrah in one fell swoop? They were sinners. Why would God tell Moses, "Speak to the congregation, saying, 'Get back from around the dwellings of Korah, Dathan and Abiram' " (Num. 16:24 NAS). Entire families were swallowed up by the earth. Sin is attractive to mankind, but the wages of sin is death.

Is such agitation and extreme urgency necessary to Christians and their lifestyles? Is there foreboding evidence which gives credibility to the call for pious living? Absolutely. "Pursue peace with all men, and the sanctification [holiness] without which no one will see the Lord" (Heb. 12:14 NAS). "Therefore, having these promises, beloved, let us cleanse ourselves from all defilement of the flesh and spirit, perfecting holiness in the fear of God" (2 Cor. 7:1 NAS).

Two Examples

Let us look more closely at two instances of sin: Dathan and Abiram, and Nadab and Abihu. Dathan and Abiram rebelled against Moses' authority with falsified arguments and anger. (See Numbers chapter 16.) Sin was committed, and it was known by the culprits. Eventually their sin affected the entire congregation of people. Moses interceded for the congregation, but Dathan, Abiram, their wives, their sons and their little ones were swallowed up when the earth opened its jaws. All because of a defiant attitude and grumbling.

We see here the sins of a few men affecting a larger group: their families. One man sins, all are guilty, especially if the sinner is in a position of leadership. "...All the men who belonged to Korah, with their possessions perished" (Num. 16:32 NAS). "Fire also came forth from the LORD and consumed the two hundred and fifty men who were offering the incense" (Num. 16:35 NAS).

In our second example, Nadab and Abihu offered "strange fire" (Lev. 10:1). This strange fire was offered "before the LORD." "And fire came out from the presence of the LORD and consumed them..." (Lev. 10:2 NAS). A lack of respect for orders and practicing worship in their own way brought immediate judgment. Divine discipline and divine justice are inseparable, and as in this case, immediate.

It was God who gave Israel their laws, government, customs and moral laws, not Moses or anyone else.

There was no allowance for them to discredit God's law in these matters.

Mankind's immaturity inexorably drives him to seek self-importance. But it will ultimately lead to his impotent exclusion, if not destruction.

The Day of the Lord

You may think your wisdom and capabilities are overlooked. Israel shares that fault with many of us today. The pattern continues. As it was with Israel, so also with us, when we withdraw from God's righteousness. The Bible often mentions the subject of "the day of the Lord...." This phrase is used at least 300 times, both in the Old Testament and the New Testament. What is revealed in context is *restoration*.

God will restore His creation which man by disobedience corrupted. It presently is in the sphere of satanic activity and will be until such time when God creates a "new heaven and a new earth...new Jerusalem" (Rev. 21:1-2 NAS).

What a day that will be! The day of the Lord is referred to either directly or by alluding to its aspects: birthpangs, wrath of God, tribulation, etc. Some scholars have proposed that this "day" or "days" will far exceed the days of woe experienced during the pogroms of Russia and the Holocaust of Germany, the time of "Jacob's trouble."

The portion of the Bible largely avoided, to the shame of the modern Church, is the Tanach, the Hebrew Bible or the Old Testament. Its exegesis is found to be richly rewarding. That is the work of the Church today. Israel was commissioned by Almighty God to perform a special work. Unfortunately, they failed. The Church is appropriately assigned *a special charge,* embodying a message for our communities, our nation and the world. Let us not fail.

The Church of Today

The message of the Church is to be one of articulation and proclamation, not one of entertainment and competition. The Church no longer sings: "The Church's one foundation is Jesus Christ, her Lord; She is His New Creation, by water and the Word" (ULCA Hymnal, 1918).

Our Church is the only one that has the ark of the covenant. We must protect our doctrines at all cost. However, Uzzah thought similarly one day when the ark was being returned to its rightful place in Jerusalem. He laid his hands on the ark and was immediately struck dead (2 Sam. 6:6-7). Let the reader cogitate on the truth expressed in this Scripture. There is throughout Scripture a "pattern" to be observed and a dogma that must be believed. You are obligated to obey, and there is objectivity in obeying His will.

Not just anyone is spiritually capable of handling the Word to the glory of God. "For we are not like many, peddling the word of God, but as from sincerity, but as from God, we speak *in Christ* in the sight of God" (2 Cor. 2:17 NAS). You say you want all that God has to offer? Can God trust you? Or are you just another who thinks like Uzzah did? If you have unconfessed uncleanness, God does not need your help.

But when you see the King, the Lord of Hosts, you will do as Isaiah did when he cried out, "...I am a man of unclean lips..." (6:5 NAS). But God touched those lips with a coal from off the altar, "and he touched my *mouth* with it and said, 'Behold, this has touched your *lips*; and your *iniquity* is taken away, and your sin is forgiven [atoned for]'" (6:7 NAS).

The churches of this day are divided as never before. Very seldom do we see a spirit of unity present in any given community. One church, assembly or denomination is not the sole possessor of the ark. There may be others not of your fold that God wants brought to Him.

Such closeness is the worst kind of myopic astigmatism that displeases the Lord. It hinders growth in the Spirit. Without the Holy Spirit, a church's growth is strangled both spiritually and numerically. Empty pews cannot pay tithes.

But there are some spiritually alive churches in the nation. Some that I know have, praise God, grown numerically in ten years to a membership of many thousands of members. These have large numbers of young people attending and in some cases have a missionary budget in the hundreds of thousands, even a few approaching one million. They have believed God, being tithers of time, talent and money.

Our Message to the World

John 3:16, Christ's word to Nicodemus, a Pharisee, a ruler of the Jews, was, "God so loved the world...."

Though the following words were not spoken, they might have been. Christ might have said, "Nicodemus, what are you going to do about it? Your forefathers did not heed My voice spoken by the prophets. I could not use them. They spent years in captivity because of disobedience. Surely God loves the world, but the world does not know that and will not know it unless you tell them. I spoke to Israel from the mountain, in the burning bush, and literally frightened them. I need someone to tell this people of My love for them."

God has done all He can ever do for the world. He sacrificed His Son and to "whosoever believeth in Him" is the promise of eternal salvation. "And there is salvation in no one else; for there is no other name under heaven that has been given among men, by which we *must* be saved" (Acts 4:12 NAS).

"...God our Savior...who desires all men to be saved and to come to the knowledge of the truth" (1 Tim. 2:3-4 NAS). God desires that all men be saved. Apparently not all will be saved; hence those not saved are unrepentant sinners, not welcome in His family. John 3:16 still stands, its message permanently invincible. Until you or I or someone whom the Holy Spirit designates witnesses to that lost soul, that person's condition is spelled out in a four letter word: lost! Did you get the message? Is your minister preaching the message?

We Must Bear Fruit

Any academic degree and ordination to the ministry is invalidated, spurious and deprived of its value or authority when no fruit is evident. Fruit bearing, or the lack of it, is strongly censored if not condemned by the Lord Jesus Himself.

In John 15:2 and 6, Christ states with unequivocal candor the requirement that fruit must be forthcoming. Matthew records that Christ speaks qualitatively, that the tree must bear "good fruit" (7:17-19). It is a frightening arraignment, and possible death warrant, where no fruit is borne. The reason there is no fruit, quite simply, is that there is no root.

In John the Baptist's ministry, recorded in Luke 3:3-20, John preached a "baptism of repentance for forgiveness of sins" (v. 3). He spoke with fervor, not from any humanist design or plan (although he calls some of his "religious" hearers "vipers"). John called for "good fruit;" for "the axe is already laid to the root of the trees..." (Luke 3:9 NAS).

All through the Scriptures the tree is used parabolically, beginning in the Garden of Eden. Trees can be a source of shelter, a supply of food and even a source of life, as in the spiritual sense of the tree of life in the Garden. Diet faddists today extol the value to the body when one eats fresh fruit.

The Holy Spirit directed three Gospel writers to the tree. When read in context, one can see providence in this "coincidence." The Heavenly Father uses the mundane to evoke from the heart His message that is intended to improve their spiritual well-being. In every mention of the tree one finds a profound teaching that is absent from many pulpits today. How long has it been since you heard someone cry out as people did to John the Baptist: "What shall we do?"

Preaching without spiritual authority is illegitimate, garbled and without profit. It is like the chaff and unfruitful branches that are fit only for the fire of judgment. Just ask those exiting a Sunday church service about the sermon. Nine out of ten won't be able to recall much, if anything. Well, you may say, "I don't want to have my head chopped off like John the Baptist." Then keep on doing what you are doing. The consequences have been announced beforehand; they follow the pattern.

15

Where Is the Church?

Every segment of society worldwide, whether sovereign, democratic, provincial or parochial, has its magisterial prerogatives: the right of precedence in its society. The precedence of authority is a moral obligation to commitment. Only then can there be a free flow of ideas that meld mankind into a well-rounded, uniform whole. It is nothing celestial or ethereal, it's just common sense for the world today.

The Bible, the believer's handbook, opens with five simple but meaningful words: "In the beginning God created…" (Gen. 1:1 NAS). He started with perfection in mind.

When God created man, He created him perfect. He was then properly advised and given free rein to move about as he saw fit with but one legally defined restriction. So in other words, man was given authority. But, man left to his own machinations and devices revealed treachery, which was transmitted to his offspring.

This happened in the very environment that God created for the enjoyment and good of all mankind.

God saw that "the wickedness of man was great on the earth, and that every intent of the *thoughts of his heart* was only evil continually" (Gen. 6:5 NAS). Was it hedonism that caused man to elicit from God so severe judgment as the Flood? No, just satan.

Satan's motivation is the same today as it was after the fall of Adam. We are constrained to say that the environment around us is in a state of chaos and dissolution with an alarming tendency to interrupt the Lord's planned sequence. Each one of us is adversely affected in a multitude of ways. In the days following the Garden of Eden, God, in a manner of speaking, "pulled the plug" and the whole mess, engineered by man, went down the drain in the Flood (Genesis 6-8).

"But as the days of Noah were, so also will the coming of the Son of Man be" (Matt. 24:37 NKJ). "...The patience of God kept waiting in the days of Noah..." (1 Pet. 3:20 NAS). When we read the newspapers, watch the television news programs and listen to the radio, we are able to draw parallels today that are, for us, alarm signals that some events of cataclysmic proportions are about to occur.

Do we have any Noahs in the pulpits who sense the urgency of the hour in which we seem to be living as carefree if not as recklessly as in Noah's day? The Church, it seems, is in quarantine, with but few exceptions.

A Definition

What is the Church? The answer to that question will arouse delirious ambiguities because in so many instances people are themselves not certain just what they mean, or how to best circumscribe the Church and its relationship to society.

The Church must be a viable countersignature of the Holy Spirit, a living organism capable of growing and developing as a seed grows and develops. Luke refreshes the memory of the disciples/apostles in his recounting: "...He [Christ] was taken up, *after* He had by the Holy Spirit given orders to the apostles *whom He had chosen*. ...to wait for what the Father had promised, 'Which,' He said, '*you heard from Me*' " (Acts 1:2, 4 NAS). The apostle John had dutifully recorded of the Holy Spirit whom the Father had promised Christ would come (John 14:16-17, 26). The fulfillment of that promise was narrated by Luke, beginning with the second chapter of Acts.

Thus is the beginning of a "new thing" alluded to in Isaiah 43:19 and 48:6 as well as in Second Corinthians 5:17. The Jews rejected their Messiah, the Lord Jesus Christ, so God by His Holy Spirit is now turning to the "wild branches" (see Romans chapter 11).

The Church, then, is the "new thing," the end result over which the Holy Spirit has jurisdiction and responsibility.

James relates how Simeon said one of God's first concerns was the "taking from the Gentiles a people for His name" (Acts 15:13-14 NAS). The call God issued to the group of believers newly formed through the Holy Spirit was that His name be propagated generation after generation.

Jesus is the Head of the Church; the believers constitute the Body. Christ is the Head and is "before all things, and in Him all things hold together" (Col. 1:17 NAS). Paul's reference in Colossians is that Christ existed prior to "all things" and that by Him all things endure. So He, as the Head of the Church, is the element in God's realm over which we have no control.

As Jesus is the Head, and we are not, so also we are the Body, and He is not. Accordingly, as the Body we meet face to face with a startling and demanding word: subjection. Paul uses it repeatedly (1 Cor. 9:27; 15:28; Gal. 2:5).

With the passing of time many have appeared saying that God had appointed them as the head of the Church. That is not so. It was for that reason Paul warned of those who would try to assert primacy in the Church. *The proprietorship of the Church belongs solely to the Holy Spirit.* The composition of the Church is made up of born again believers.

That particular word, then, is for those who are His children. You are everything to God that Christ is (1 John 4:17). For when you were born again you were not one-half or one-quarter born again. You did not become one-half righteous or one-quarter righteous. God did a perfect work in you and Paul calls this fact to the attention of the Church in his day (Phil. 3:15 KJV). The word "perfect" translated from the Greek *telios* means "completeness" and "perfection." That word conjures up in us all manner of negatives and denials. The Lord has generous grace for those who demand to be inferior to the pattern or standard He set forth as that which is "well-pleasing" in His sight (1 Cor. 10:5; Col. 1:10; 3:20; 1 Thess. 2:15; 4:1; 1 John 3:22).

The Church's Condition

What is the condition of the Church today? Obviously some alteration in manner and quality of the Church's contact with those outside the fold has occurred. Those who gather statistical information related to church attendance or church membership say that the Church is losing ground. In other words, there continues to be a marked erosion of members from the churches' rolls, while at the same time the cultic community—the New Age, the Muslims, the Hari Krishnas, Jehovah's Witnesses and others—is growing.

Unfortunately, the juxtaposition between pulpit and pew in many, less firmly established churches is widening. This attitude prevails among many members in the Church that the prize is meager and not worth the cost. What is the prize? Paul in Philippians 3:14 said, "I press on toward the goal for *the prize* of the upward call of God in Christ Jesus" (NAS).

What was the price in Zechariah's day? "So they weighed out thirty shekels of silver...Then the LORD said to me, 'Throw it to the potter, that magnificent price at which I was valued by them' " (Zech. 11:12b-13a NAS). Today tithing is perhaps shared by hardly more than *ten* percent of most congregations. The potter syndrome prevails more today perhaps than ever before. The Lord, obviously, is grieved and the nongiver has lost his blessing of the opened windows of heaven (Mal. 3:10).

Leadership Today

What is to be the demeanor, the outward manner or the comportment of the pulpit in this day? The person assigned or chosen to serve at the "sacred desk" has a responsibility of awesome proportions, and is often resigned to loneliness. Perseverance and dedication are necessary as you minister to the needs of the people, desiring to stimulate a resourcefulness similar to that of the prophetess Anna.

Let's look at this Anna, the prophetess. She was a daughter of Phanuel [trans. the face of God], of the tribe of Asher [trans. happy]. She had only seven years of marriage before her husband died. Was that the end? No, she lived to be 84 years old, and she was happy in what she did: She served in the temple night and day with fasting and prayers, giving thanks to God and looking for the redemption of Israel. She never left the temple. One of her contemporaries was Simeon, [trans. hearing, or to hear intelligently], and because he heard, this righteous and devout man was also looking for the consolation of Israel (Luke 2:36; 2:25 NAS).

That should cause a light to start flashing. Here we have the presentation of Jesus in the temple, the shekinah glory of God visiting the temple for the first time after being absent for so many centuries. You ask why?

Israel, God's choice, was guilty of gross disobedience and whoredoms. The prophet Ezekiel (and his contemporaries) repeatedly called these sins to the people's attention. Ezekiel chapters 4 through 11 graphically states the siege of Jerusalem and its desolation. Their idolatrous worship and wickedness would invade. The Temple would be profaned by its myriad abominations and concurrent slaughter and would cause the shekinah glory to depart the premises. Yes, the physical temple remained standing until the invasion of the armies of Babylon reduced the temple to ruin. But the temple without the guiding force was without power or meaning after the glory left.

May we be privileged to draw a parallel here and suggest that the twentieth century Church incorporates many of the traits found in Israel's conduct and that may be one of the many reasons for the Church's powerlessness.

So God demands a devotion and dedication similar to Anna's from each one of His children, beginning with the pulpit.

God Himself intervened many times when Moses faced insurmountable problems with the children of

Israel on their way to the Promised Land. Moses was commanded to tell Israel the four things required of them: "...give earnest heed to the voice of the LORD Your God, and do what is right in His sight, and give ear to all His commandments, and keep all His statutes..." (Ex. 15:26 NAS). And, if I read my Bible correctly, these were stated before God actually presented the Ten Commandments. God was priming the people, getting them ready beforehand.

Even before the law was given, Moses' father-in-law "heard of all that God had done for Moses... And Moses told his father-in-law all that the LORD had done for Israel's sake, all the hardship that had befallen them on the journey, and how the LORD had delivered them" (Ex. 18:1, 8 NAS). While Jethro visited, he observed certain irregularities in Moses' administration and counseled him on how to distribute responsibility among others (vv. 17-23).

Certifiable data relating to Moses' success as a leader were enlarged upon and had to be enforced for covenant blessings to be shared. Israel's misconduct should have warned Moses that something was out of "synch" with his people and his leadership.

Moses was God's man and God was going before them in the pillar of fire by night and the cloud by day (Ex. 13:21). Even so the people were persistently "quarreling" and "grumbling" (Ex. 17:2-3 NAS). The people did not believe Moses, whereupon he "cried out to the LORD, saying, 'What shall I do to this people? A little more and they will stone me'" (Ex.

17:4 NAS). Had it not been for Jethro, Moses might later have been "stoned." Moses' governance might have been singularly enriching for all concerned, but his conduct bespoke unreasoned judgment. He was "living too close to the trees and could not see the forest."

That phenomenon is present in our day, in the political, social and, of all places, the Church community. Where are the Jethros of our day who can, with reasoned judgment, provide theopneustic or God-breathed counsel?

The Church's Orders of the Day

The Church has consistently maintained a leisurely affirmation of the faith. The Church seems oblivious to the needs of not only itself, but also society at large. The Church has dilly-dallied with the specifics of the assignment God gave us: "Go ye therefore, and teach all nations..." (Matt. 28:29 KJV). These are the orders of the day. Is the authority of Scripture old-fashioned and out of date? Has the gospel lost its currency or novelty? A thousand times no! Where is the pride of grace, the pride of place, where we are called to serve? Stagnation and inactivity, with little or no purpose in life, the result of not knowing who God is or who you are, is a paltry, passive resistance to the evils of today.

God did not save us only so we could go to Heaven. Our armed services do not recruit men and women just to wear the uniform of the United States. Their camaraderie and cohesiveness is proudly manifested with positive compliance to the "order of the day." Every one of us will profit immeasurably when the Church objectively conforms to the cadence and pace of its marching orders.

The prophet Isaiah said, "For the Lord GOD will help me; therefore shall I not be confounded: therefore have I set my face like a *flint*, and I know that I shall not be ashamed" (Isa. 50:7 KJV). "As an adamant [*shamiyr*, Heb.; "to guard, protect"] harder than *flint* have I made thy forehead: fear them not, neither be dismayed at their looks, though they be a rebellious house" (Ezek. 3:9 KJV).

What both Isaiah and Ezekiel are saying is that God has a message to be delivered, not at all easy. But when a laissez-faire attitude prevails among His people, someone must be the mouthpiece.

Our identification, as believers, is with the Lord of Lords, the King of Kings and more especially, the Lord of Hosts or the Lord of the armies. No slackening of purpose is allowed within the ranks of God's servicemen and women. "We've a story to tell to the Nations" (Meth. Hymnal, 1963 ed.).

Problems Start Small

What is seen in the pews is the result of what comes from the pulpit. The people in the pew are scarcely interested in, nor are they helped spiritually by, atrophied preacher phrases. The preacher himself must be motivated by scriptural principles before he can maximize fruit-bearing in the branches. When the word from the pulpit inculcates, or teaches and thereby impresses by frequent repetition and admonition, the message of the Trinity of the Godhead, the virgin birth and eternity, you will find that this methodology transcends all plans devised by mere man.

The phrase "order in the court" is heard in the courtroom when it needs to restore control. That might be appropriate language for the Church.

Since all that is true, and I believe it to be true, how did the nation, the Church and the family "fall so far from grace"? We as a people are at a time of unprecedented reliance on the social sciences. The voice of the Church has been overwhelmed by tradition and humanistic philosophies (or "foolosophy"). In an increasingly bureaucratic nation, the parents' rights are disregarded. Political sources of liberalism are in the forefront. It is little wonder that parents find that the government-controlled school system is less and less tolerant of parental prerogatives.

And why not? Just 30 years ago, 80 percent of our children grew up with both parents at home. But now we are in the "Age of the Expert." Watch your television programs—families are turning away from biblical values and traditional Christian concepts toward psychiatrists and the social sciences for help in handling the frightening problems of life in this "modern age." Check out the psychiatric facilities for the amount of teenage admissions into them. Someone advances the figure at more than 250 thousand such admissions.

So we have kids on drugs, disintegrating families and a murder center in the capital of the country. Our country abounds in teen pregnancies. Distorted, unbiblical behavior is being introduced into law, such as homosexual marriages. Libertarianism is rampant in society. "Anything goes" was the phrase heard in the past; now it's "everything goes."

Unfortunately, "everything goes" is also becoming the norm in the Church. Many can attest to the Church today being a far cry from the one of their childhood. We used to respect the house of worship. We used to have clothes we wore only for church.

To some that may seem unimportant, but it may be the beginning of a moral and spiritual breakdown. A breakdown always starts with the miniscule, but develops into something of greater significance. Laxity in communication of truth will encourage a jaundiced compliance to the pattern.

One Roman Catholic priest in a midwestern city had issued a ruling, prior to the sacrament of the Lord's Supper, or Eucharist, that everyone who partakes of the sacrament should be properly clothed. There had been those who knew the priest's ruling, but with a defiant attitude came to the services dressed (or undressed) in "shorts, bare midriffs, tank tops, jeans and sweat shirts." I am in agreement with the priest who refused to serve those people.

Now I am about to stir up some animus among some in the Christian community, for when one speaks, even softly, about manners and mannerisms, he is in trouble.

Without my saying too much more about clothes for church services, or anywhere else, let's hear what the Scriptures say. "But let all things be done properly and in an orderly manner" (1 Cor. 14:40 NAS). "Likewise, I want women to adorn themselves with proper clothing, modestly and discreetly..." (1 Tim. 2:9 NAS). But clothing is not a New Testament teaching alone. Deuteronomy 22:5 says: "A woman shall not wear man's clothing, nor shall a man put on a woman's clothing; for whoever does these things is an *abomination* to the LORD your God" (NAS). Zephaniah 1:8 says that "all who clothe themselves with foreign garments" would be punished (NAS). In today's environment, when following a couple down a street you sometimes wonder, "Which one is the female?"

Such seemingly little things do matter. "Catch the foxes for us, the little foxes that are ruining the vineyards, while our vineyards are in blossom" (Song 2:15 NAS).

All through the Scriptures, especially in the Old Testament, the Levitical priesthood and all others approaching the Temple areas were to be attired "according to the pattern."

It must be stated unequivocally that God does not force you to do what is against your will. However, it must also be said that the blessing of God upon your life is contingent upon obedience to His will for your sake.

Peroration

The Severity of Jesus' Reprimand (Judgments)

Paul's concern for believers in his day reflected the precepts or authoritative commands of the prophetic Scriptures and of the Lord Jesus. Reprimands from Paul as well as from the Lord Jesus were not uncommon. Their judgments were at times personal and at times political in their outreach, and they were without exemption.

Christ's words in John 7:24 were to judge correctly. At another time in His colloquy with Peter (Luke 7:43), He says "You have judged correctly" (NAS). Again with Peter, Jesus says, "And why do you not even on your own initiative judge what is right?" (Luke 12:57 NAS).

Judgment seems to accelerate action in the individual's response; more especially in the life of the believer. The matter of judgment puzzles many within the household of God, notwithstanding the commanding tone of Paul's word to the Corinthian church. "But he who is spiritual appraises [judges] all things, yet he himself is appraised by no man" (1 Cor. 2:15 NAS). In 10:15 of the same epistle, Paul says, "I speak as to wise men; you judge what I say" (NAS).

Paul in Romans 16:17 echoes a familiar word of caution: "Now I urge you, brethren, keep your eye on those who cause dissensions and hindrances [occasions of stumbling] contrary to the teaching which you learned, and turn away from them" (NAS).

Because little or no judgmental verbiage is heard in our day from the pulpit, the Church is in a state of apathy and inertia. Sin has lost its meaning. The severity of the judgment of God is not known.

The familiar verse quoted from Matthew 7:1-5 needs to be examined in the light of its context. When a person does so, he or she can readily see that the message is directed to the hypocrite (v. 5). Whenever a text is lifted from its context, there follows in rapid succession a corruption of Scripture's intent.

The Church is honeycombed with and paralyzed by humanistic philosophies. It has assumed doctrinaire theories as scriptural fact.

Spiritual health is maintained by rejecting, and by separating oneself from, the germ of false doctrine.

In Paul's day heretical theories were diffused throughout the land. So there was a constant call to be watchful and to judge all things by the prophetic word.

In our day the same sense of urgency prevails, to be faithful as in the prophets' day (Hos. 2:19-20). But we see the house of worship forsaken, the sacraments neglected. People dividing into sects put off, as it were, the garment of praise for the ashes of judgment.

History records that when the Jews became more and more divided and confused, the tyranny of the Roman Empire increased. There followed great slaughter of the Jews and the confiscation of their property.

John the Baptist preached a message at the time of the great slaughter of babies under Herod. His message was repentance; but it was unconditionally rejected and ultimately cost John his head (Matt. 14:8).

Is there perhaps a correlation today with the slaughter of the unborn numbering in the millions? No one knows how many babies Herod ordered killed, but as in those days, so also in the waning years of this twentieth century. We as a people in America are facing dire and ominous judgment and the potential for a destruction similar to the fall of the Roman Empire.

The Roman Empire was not very cordial to the preaching of the gospel; Paul was beheaded and Peter was hanged, and that was but the tip of the iceberg.

The work of the ministry is presented throughout Scripture as dangerous to one's health, especially so if one's dedication and devotion is genuinely resolute and with a decided purpose to serve God for His name's sake.

For the present, the Church is in a kindergarten syndrome, unfortunately.

The purpose of this author is to call attention to the obvious disarrangement [or derangement] within the organized, corporate church. That has had deleterious influence upon society locally and at large. If the Church has no identifiable future, how can one expect the *vox populi* to be anything but confused, frustrated and angry?